DIFFICULT GIFTS

Difficult Gifts

A physician's journey
to heal body and mind

COURTNEY BURNETT

Minneapolis

ISBN 13: 978-1-63489-409-8

Library of Congress Catalog Number has been applied for.
Printed in the United States of America
First Printing: 2021

25   24   23   22   21   5   4   3   2   1

Cover design by Holly Ovendon
Interior design by Patrick Maloney

Wise Ink Creative Publishing
807 Broadway St NE
Suite 46
Minneapolis, MN, 55413

To order, visit www.itascabooks.com or call 1-800-901-3480.
Reseller discounts available.

To Nora: may you always find beauty in life's little moments.

Contents

Prologue

There are only two days in the year that nothing can be done.
One is called yesterday and the other is called tomorrow.
Today is the right day to love, believe, do, and mostly live.

—the Dalai Lama

The story you are about to read is true. It is a raw, honest, intimate narration of the most unexpected time in my life.

I have malignant, aggressive brain cancer, and it will likely kill me someday. Despite this, I am happy. I am filled with joy, love, compassion, and gratitude for every moment of life I am living. This was definitely not always the case.

Six months prior to the writing of this book, I was a healthy twenty-nine-year-old resident physician finishing a three-year residency in internal medicine. I had been nominated and selected to work as a chief resident after graduation. I had published scientific papers and received strong letters of recommendation, and I had job offers lined up.

However, despite professional success, I was miserable. I was clinically depressed, unhappy, and facing a failing marriage.

As a physician, I had spent nearly my entire adult life working toward the goal of becoming an independently practicing doctor. I had tirelessly studied in college, graduated with honors and a major in genetics, worked my ass off to gain acceptance to medical school, and continued to study aggressively with the goal of matching into my first-choice residency. I lived my life as if I were running a marathon, always looking for the finish line, without ever noticing the beautiful scenery around me. Physicians will often tell you that we are artists in the field of delayed gratification. We run and run, often tired, often stumbling, always self-critical, in hopes of reaching an overly glorified finish line. We spend years in school, residency, and sub-specialty training, making little money, working long hours, and dedicating ourselves tirelessly to the pursuit of the "end goal"—the time when a physician is finally qualified to work as an independently practicing doctor.

I had run for a long time. The finish line was in sight for me—only six months of clinical rotations and a chief residency year, and my dream of becoming an independently practicing doctor would be granted.

Why, then, was I so unhappy? I could not answer this question. Instead, I began to write a novel. It was a new adventure for me; I thought a creative outlet would help me explore and understand my sadness. I crafted a plot revolving around a young woman whose mind was playing tricks on her. I had written around one hundred pages of what I thought was a fairly decent first novel when the time came for me to travel to Thailand for a global health rotation.

Life works in mysterious ways. Four weeks later, I was having the time of my life in Thailand when I started to experience strange neurological symptoms.

Since I'm dying, I'll get right to the point—my trip did not go as planned. My strange symptoms turned out to be seizures, and while I was still in Thailand, I diagnosed myself with a brain tumor. As you will soon read in much more detail, this brain tumor turned out to be aggressive brain cancer, and my life was changed forever.

I started writing a blog when I was first diagnosed as a helpful and therapeutic way to keep family and friends back home updated. I noticed that when I would update friends on the phone, the majority of the conversation would consist of people saying

"I'm so sorry. This isn't fair." I would respond with reassurance, trying to console them in their grief and guilt for not being with me during this time. Phone calls became exhausting. Rather than continuing them, I returned to writing, posting a chapter on my blog every few days for months. These months included an emergency medical flight home from Thailand to the United States, two intensive brain surgeries, chemotherapy, radiation, a divorce, a deepening exploration of my Buddhist spirituality, and a global pandemic. Sounds like a good story, doesn't it? Too bad for me that it's entirely nonfiction.

I soon realized that my real-life story was far more exciting than the fictional story I had been writing. I never in my wildest dreams imagined that my words or my story could inspire others, could help relieve them of their own suffering or help them find happiness despite the inevitable chaos of life. Quite unexpectedly, my blog gained a worldwide following. Readers told me that my words had inspirational, profound effects on them. One even told me that my blog posts contained "more helpful information than any therapist, life coach, or mentor ever gave me," which completely and utterly blew my mind. This reader, among many others, inspired me to transform my blog's short stories into a book.

Without this memoir, I imagine I would still be curled up in bed in the fetal position, crying about the horrendous fate life brought me. Fortunately, I am not. The book you are about to read is my true story of developing a meaningful and compassionate life while battling malignant brain cancer; or really, while battling the suffering that life brings to all of us when we least want or expect it.

This story may interest you, inspire you, help you, calm you, encourage you, or scare you, but regardless, I hope it makes you feel something. Writing this book allowed me to cope with an overwhelming situation—with the realization that the future is completely out of our control, no matter how much we try to plan otherwise.

Whatever your greatest obstacle is—cancer, physical illness, pain, poverty, depression, anxiety, social injustice, fear of failure, fear of loneliness, or one of the many millions of other obstacles this human life is guaranteed to give us—I hope my story encourages you to embrace life despite it all.

Even though my story may at first seem somewhat unique, really, it is not. I am simply a human being trying my best to overcome suffering and find happiness, as we all are every day of our lives. I have learned the greatest gift I can offer is the simple understanding that none of us face this messy life alone. We are all connected. We are all human. We are all simply trying to be happy, and we all deserve that happiness.

When I think about the basic facts of life, I believe all human beings are similar. We are born, we experience emotions, we face challenges, we learn something, we age, we grow ill, and we die. I find it interesting that so many of us do not like to think or talk about aging, illness, or death, even though every single one of us has our mortality in common.

Sometimes, I reflect on my recent experiences and wonder if all this happened to allow me to help others in a more meaningful way than I ever dreamed possible. I initially envisioned doing this as a physician, and I still will, while I can.

Through dying, I have learned to live. Through sadness, I have found happiness. Through the loss of the guaranteed future I once envisioned, I have found peace and freedom. I am more alive today than I have ever been.

This book is called *Difficult Gifts* because that is what cancer has been to me. Cancer saved my life. Cancer is the most difficult, beautiful, life-changing gift I have ever received.

I don't know how much time I have left on this earth, but while I'm still here, I invite you to come on an honest, sometimes painful, but mostly beautiful glimpse into my world. I promise to tell you my story with complete honesty and truth in the way that

I know it. I have, however, changed some names and identifying details to protect the privacy of others in the stories that follow.

I am grateful beyond belief that, despite the unexpected challenges life has given me, I am able to use my words to help others in even the smallest of ways. I hope my story will motivate you to embrace this moment and find happiness in even the most difficult of gifts.

1

The departure

Be kind whenever possible. It is always possible.

—the Dalai Lama

There are many places I could start this story, but I'm going to start it in January of 2020, when I found myself standing alone in a long security line at the Minneapolis–St. Paul International Airport, waiting to board a flight to Chiang Mai, Thailand. At the time, I did not know that I would return home from Thailand with a newly discovered brain tumor in my right frontal lobe and a very new outlook on life.

As I stood in a seemingly never-ending line, I reflected on the strange course of events that had led me to the present moment. A few months prior, I had applied for a global health elective. My medical residency program at the University of Minnesota offered a number of global health elective rotations to choose from, but I had instantly been drawn to Thailand, where I would have the opportunity to practice traditional and complementary medicine at a small clinic in urban Chiang Mai.

I was very fortunate to train at the University of Minnesota, whose fantastic medical residency program was filled with brilliant minds, fascinating patients, incredible teachers, and endless educational opportunities. I had spent years cultivating my passions in medical education and had recently been selected to spend a year postgraduation working as a chief medical resident, a near-peer teacher and mentor for other resident physicians. Being selected for this position was an honor, and I felt it would offer me an opportunity to expand my skill set in medical education prior to starting my full-fledged career. I had worked tirelessly to organize this professional path over much of my adult life. I was a type-A, neurotic life-planner and finally had my dream plans outlined in front of me. I could see the future. I knew exactly what was coming (ha!) and was excited beyond belief.

Yet despite professional success, at the time of my application for the global health elective, I was depressed, facing a failing marriage, and unsure how to find happiness in the life I had created for myself. I vividly remember one wintery weekend during my second year of residency: I'd returned home from the grocery store, carried my bags inside, and fallen into a crumpled, emotional heap on the cold wood floor as frozen food melted around me. Too sad, too hopeless to move, I lay on the floor next to disgusting, thawing groceries.

Thankfully, between medication, a fantastic therapist, and spiritual exploration, the fog of depression gradually lifted. Emotional freedom brought with it a new perspective on life. I found more acceptance of myself and my own limitations. I also acknowledged that my marriage was not working. My now-ex-husband James is an optimistic and peaceful man, always content, rarely rattled. I was perpetually in awe of these qualities. I loved every year of our wonderful relationship; however, the emotional chasm between us grew wider and deeper until neither of us could jump across to the other side without falling in completely.

As I gradually learned to find happiness in myself, I had to lean in toward me and further away from the bond that had once held me and James so tightly together. After five years of marriage and months of trying to fix what was irreparably broken, we separated, remaining wonderful friends to this day.

As I stood on my own in the security line, slowly inching my way toward the TSA agent ahead, I thought about how just a few short months ago, when James and I were trying to make things work, he had almost bought a ticket to come to Thailand with me. Now, I realized how happily free and independent I felt—I was alone, but not in any way lonely. I was unbelievably excited to travel to a new place, learn about another culture, explore my own spirituality, and meet new friends. I had no idea quite how transformative this journey would be, yet I like to think that some small, subconscious part of me knew that my life was about to change. Something deep inside told me that this was my time—time to explore myself and the world with every freedom life could offer. My chance to find joy, even in the most unexpected of ways.

I thought back to the day James and I had formally separated, which had happened to be my twenty-ninth birthday. Shortly after our separation, I'd nervously rented myself a moving truck and walked through our home, filled with picturesque yet superficial memories of a happy marriage, packing up my belongings. I'd sobbed as I drove myself to a new, overpriced apartment a few miles away. And then, unloading my boxes into the one-bedroom apartment where I would live alone for the first time in my adult life, I had looked around and felt myself unexpectedly smiling.

As I inched closer to the security gate, I found myself smiling once again, momentarily forgetting the past, ignoring my fears of the future, and simply living in the unique moment I had created. I was about to begin a journey of a lifetime. I had survived my first of many difficult gifts: depression and divorce. Although unpleasant at the time, without them, I would not have been standing in that security line, waiting to board a flight that would change my life forever.

2

When a book hits you on the head, read the damn book

My religion is very simple. My religion is kindness.

—the Dalai Lama

"Next, please," a cranky middle-aged man with a TSA badge yelled at me, shaking me out of my memories and back into reality. I approached the badged agent and showed him my passport, smiling nervously until he gave me the nod of approval to proceed.

The continent of Asia was new to me as a solo traveler. Apart from the delicious Thai dishes I frequently enjoyed in my home state of Minnesota, Thailand itself was a mystery to me. I was interested in learning more about Eastern and complementary medicine; I'd picked my global health elective in Thailand for the opportunity to learn Thai massage, acupuncture, and other traditional Eastern medical methods to supplement my knowledge of Western medical practices. I believe a good physician is a well-rounded physician. Science and evidence-based medicine are key components of my practice; however, there is more to the field of medicine than science can fully explain. Medicine involves humanity, birth and death, consciousness, relationships, suffering, joy, and relief; it is an art as well as a science.

"Arms overhead," a young TSA agent told me as I entered the body scanner. Cleared to proceed, I found my shoes, jacket, liquids, and computer and stuffed them quickly back inside my suitcase.

As I arrived at my gate, I realized I had nearly an hour before my flight departed. I sat down in a sun-drenched, sticky blue chair and decided to give my parents a call to let them know my flight was on time.

I am very close with my parents and knew I would miss them terribly while away. My mother, Mary, is an angel of a woman. An extremely successful attorney and mediator, she's nevertheless one of the humblest people I know. She speaks with a soft, calm air about her, cautiously and intelligently choosing her words as useful tools, never weapons. My father, Ken, is a hardworking entrepreneur type with endless skills. He has been an attorney, a pilot, a flight instructor, an architect, an accountant, an investment banker, and other things I likely still have yet to learn. He can fix anything you put in front of him and still can't understand why I hired someone to install a garbage disposal when we could have done it ourselves.

My mom answered on the first ring. "Hi, honey!"

"Hi, Mom. Is Dad around?"

This was followed by the familiar click of the speakerphone turning on. "Hey, Court! Make it to your gate?" my dad yelled from across the room.

"I'm here. Flight leaves in an hour. I'm going to grab a coffee and kill some time," I told them.

"Well, we miss you already. Let us know when you arrive safely. We love you." I heard my mom hold back a quiet sniffle. Agreeing with her, I hung up the phone as I drifted back into my memories.

My parents met in their early thirties at a law firm in Minneapolis. They had two children, me and my younger brother, Matt. Matt is, simply put, the best human being I know; he's one of my best friends and always has been. He has the perfect combination of my mother and father's personalities; he is a humble genius who I strongly believe can do anything. Three years younger than I am, he's a captain and pilot in the US Army, a West Point graduate, and a hero.

Growing up, we lived in a nice home in a peaceful suburb. I had a beautiful, privileged upbringing; however, I never quite felt like I fit in with my peers. I was teased relentlessly growing up: for my silly-shaped nose, my poor athletic skills, my social anxiety, and my overall shy personality. For years, I was scared to go to school, to sit on the bus, to eat lunch in the cafeteria. My social anxiety was high, and I was in many ways a loner. I longed for acceptance yet didn't know how to find it. To be honest, I don't think I realized until quite recently that the only person I really need acceptance from is myself.

In grade school, I was the smart kid, the kid who left her second-grade class to study algebra with the fifth-graders, the kid whose teacher brought in a stack of literature for her to read in the corner while her first-grade peers read picture books. I was the girl who spent free time sitting in the library instead of running around on the playground. I am still this kid, honestly, only now, I love the role.

"Thirty minutes until boarding," the gate agent yelled harshly into the speakers overhead. Startled, I rushed to the nearest Starbucks to grab a coffee and sat back down in my sticky blue chair, pulling out a book from my suitcase: *The Universe in a Single Atom: The Convergence of Science and Spirituality.* I was incredibly excited to start reading this book, which had entered my life unexpectedly and quite literally by force.

A few days before my flight, I had been wandering through a local bookstore on the way to my typical Sunday evening yoga class. I was particularly nervous about this yoga class because my instructor had warned me that a headstand would be involved. I had practiced yoga for many years but always had great fear about inversions, particularly headstands. I had never tried one; I couldn't imagine the embarrassment I would feel falling out of a headstand in front of a class of fit, perfectly balanced yogis. Unfortunately, my new single lifestyle brought with it the development of an extreme crush on my yoga instructor. I wanted to leave him with a beautiful memory of me executing a perfect headstand before leaving for my month in Thailand.

I worked on headstands for days leading up to the class, practicing in my apartment, at the gym, at the yoga studio. I fell more times than I can count, and I laughed at myself often. Eventually, I managed one. Then I did another, then another, and soon the headstands came naturally. It was as if I could not remember ever not knowing how to do a headstand. How strange, I thought, that our bodies are limited so intensely by our minds.

After far too many hours spent on headstand practice, I felt confident I would be able to perfect my new skill in class. I put on my most stylish yoga gear, left home too early, and stopped at a bookstore on the way. It was just to kill some time, I told myself—under no circumstances was I allowed to purchase any more books. I love to read, but I needed a book-purchasing hiatus for the health of my bank account and bookshelf.

While in this bookstore, standing next to a small shelf of Buddhist literature, I picked up the Dalai Lama's book *The Universe in a Single Atom: The Convergence of Science and Spirituality* and curiously read the back cover. "The Dalai Lama presents a brilliant analysis of why all avenues of inquiry—science as well as spiritual—must be pursued in order to arrive at a complete picture of the truth." This description spoke to me. I love the idea of merging thoughts, ideas, experiments, and questions from multiple different areas of study to see how they all interact.

Spirituality, science, and Buddhism all in one title? I needed this book. But I had promised myself I would not buy one, so I put it back on the shelf above me and started to back away.

THUMP.

Ouch. I touched the spot where *The Universe in a Single Atom* had fallen off the shelf and hit me smack on the right side of my head, the exact spot a tumor would be found one month later.

Luckily, I took this very strange, very direct book's whispering seriously. *Well, I guess I can buy just one book today.* I grabbed that haunted book, raced to the register, and purchased it as fast as I possibly could. I don't usually believe in signs, but this was one. I was mesmerized by this book and thanked it profusely for hitting me on the head. In fact, I still do. That day I learned: when a book hits you on the head, you should probably read the damn book.

Opening the first page of this mesmerizing book at Gate C6 and sipping my steaming hot dark-roast coffee, I reflected on the strange path I'd taken to find my Buddhist spirituality. My parents raised Matt and me as Catholics. My father was himself raised Catholic, and my mother was brought up in a Methodist household. Both of my parents felt an upbringing incorporating formal religious training had value, and my mother agreed with my father to raise her children as Catholic. My father's extended family was pleased with this decision.

Matt and I were baptized, encouraged to attend religious classes, and confirmed as teenagers. I often told my parents I did not want to go to church with them. I longed from an early age to learn about other religions. I wanted to mix things up, to spend one Sunday at the Catholic church and the next week in the Jewish synagogue. I craved variety and challenged the lessons Catholicism taught.

For starters, I have always been a strong feminist, even from a very young age. I thank my mother for this—while she's too humble to necessarily call herself a feminist, she is absolutely the epitome of a badass woman who can do absolutely anything with graceful humility. As a young feminist, I could not comprehend the lack of female leadership within the Catholic Church. Why was the priest a man? Why were all the other church leaders men? Why did the nuns have to sit together in a pew in the back while the men led the service? This angered me as a child because I didn't understand. Honestly, it still angers me a little now.

This was not the only piece of Catholicism that irked me. The list of suspect curiosities piled up in my childhood mind, and I found myself getting angry at my parents quite often for insisting I go to Catholic church every Sunday. Looking back, I understand now that my parents were doing what seemed right at the time. They raised their children in a faith that was exceptionally important to them; it had raised them, their parents before them, and so on. This faith was not challenged or questioned by anyone in our family over generations, until a strange little girl with a quirky brain came along and began to shake things up.

I respect all religions, very much, and I do not mean to imply that Catholicism is in some way wrong. To be as honest as possible, I tell you this story from my past because Catholicism did not fit my own personal values. I found no inspiration in Catholicism, no peace, no understanding of something greater. This led me to abandon religion for a number of years once I moved out of my parents' home for college, until I found Buddhism during residency.

In residency, I was introduced to the writings of Pema Chödrön, an incredible Buddhist nun and spiritual teacher. The philosophy and teachings of the Dharma, or Buddhist scripture, resonated with me. I quickly found myself meditating, participating in a local Sangha (Buddhist community), and finding extraordinary happiness through the writings of many inspirational teachers, including His Holiness the Fourteenth Dalai Lama, Pema Chödrön, Sharon Salzberg, Thich Nhat Hanh, and many others. Within a few months, I had a bookshelf filled with Buddhist literature: books I underlined, took notes in, and read until the pages literally fell out and were scattered across my apartment. I found absolute joy in Buddhism. The Dharma changed my life in ways Catholicism never could.

I personally believe the ultimate purpose of religion is to help us each find love, kindness, compassion, and community. For me,

Buddhism did these things. My spirituality became an increasingly important aspect of my life over the upcoming months, months filled with unbelievable amounts of suffering. Without Buddhism, I don't think I would have survived. I claim no expertise in any of the Buddhist concepts I will discuss in my story. I know I am simply beginning to learn about a spirituality, a religion, a lifestyle which many others have dedicated their lives to studying and understanding. I do not write about Buddhism to popularize or push a belief system on others. I write about Buddhism because it saved my life, simple as that.

The messages I have found most inspirational are not exclusive to Buddhism. They are universal concepts of love, of compassion, of the ability to overcome our suffering and experience happiness during our short time on this earth. I do not wish to offend anyone and surely do not wish to profit on these deeply spiritual, centuries-old ideas for my own benefit. My ultimate wish in this life, which will likely be shorter than I originally expected, is to help others. This is why I became a physician; this is why I wrote a book. By serving others, I find purpose.

I am very sure my interpretations of the Buddhist texts I will quote throughout this book simply touch at a thin surface of a subject experts have worked years to master. All I can say is, opening my mind to a new way of thinking about spirituality brought me happiness and joy during my life's darkest times.

༄

"Now boarding," the overhead speaker told me, shaking me out of my thoughts. Stuffing my book back into my suitcase, I stood in line to get on the plane, ready to start a journey that would change my life in ways still unimaginable to me.

3

Arriving in Thailand

If we want a genuine smile, then first we must
produce the basis for a smile to come.

—the Dalai Lama

After over thirty hours of traveling, including three separate flights and a questionably named fish rice meal served for breakfast, I landed in Chiang Mai. Stepping out of the plane into the CNX airport, I breathed in smells of sweaty travelers, dusty luggage, old coffee, airline fuel, and adventure. I had never felt more alive.

I was terrified that my checked luggage had wound up stuck somewhere between Minnesota and Thailand. Fortunately, after watching the luggage carousel rotate for what felt like hours, I eventually spied my two large suitcases. Letting out a sigh of relief, I wheeled my bags behind me while I looked for my name on a private driver's handwritten sign. Before my arrival, I had found a gorgeous rental apartment online. My kind host had told me she'd arranged for a private driver to take me from the airport to my apartment when I arrived.

My driver, a short, friendly looking man, clasped his hands together as if in prayer, bowed to me, and smiled. I quickly learned he did not speak one word of English, and I did not speak one word of Thai. I was terribly ashamed of myself for not spending more time learning the native language prior to my arrival.

We drove silently for twenty minutes through urban Chiang Mai, passing an unbelievable number of adorable cafés, elegant

Buddhist temple grounds filled with monks in saffron-colored robes, and universities brimming with students sitting outside enjoying the bright, sunny day. Occasionally, I glanced down at a small, silly-looking bobblehead Buddha statue on the dashboard of the car. Buddha seemed to be smiling at me, saying, *"You're about to have quite an unexpected adventure here!"* I smiled back foolishly. Oh, how naïve I was.

After a very quiet drive, we reached a slightly run-down apartment building on the edge of Nimmanhaemin Road, a busy central thoroughfare running through the heart of Chiang Mai. It was filled with apartments, hotels, boutique shops, massage salons, restaurants, and hundreds of people.

Although a bit derelict on the exterior, the apartment complex backed up against Doi Suthep mountain. Wat Phra That Doi Suthep, a beautiful and sacred Buddhist temple dating back to the fourteenth century, sat high on one of the mountain's peaks. Its gold-plated chedi, or spherical dome-like structure, shone down on the city of Chiang Mai below. I had never seen anything more beautiful.

My driver stopped the car, and a young woman walked over to greet me with a smile. She bowed to me in a similar prayer-like fashion and introduced herself in hesitant English as my host. She escorted me to my apartment, which to my surprise was significantly more beautiful than the neglected exterior.

I walked into a bright, sparkling-clean kitchen flooded with natural light from three large windows. The unit had two bedrooms (each with a luxurious king-sized bed, a true extravagance while traveling abroad), a sun-filled living room, and a bathroom complete with a deep-soaker bathtub. I thanked my host and bowed to her in what was likely a very foolish way. After she left my bedroom, I set down my luggage, flopped onto one of the glorious beds, and let out a squeal of pure joy. I had arrived.

An hour after arriving at my new, gloriously chic apartment, I found myself still smiling as I lay on the large, comfortable bed. Despite jet lag, I needed to explore the magical place around me. I found my touristy map of Chiang Mai, changed into a sundress, doused myself in bug spray, and ventured out to find dinner under the lights of this lively, bustling city.

I found myself stopping to look and smell endless delicious foods on my way down busy Nimmanhaemin Road. Street food is everywhere in Thailand. Passing a small roadside market, I stopped to look at and smell stacks of skewered meat, glistening and oily, making my mouth water. "*Sawatdee-ka*," an elderly female vendor said to me.

"Hi," I muttered. Blushing, I attempted a full "Sawatdee-ka" back to her, bowing in prayer as I had learned was customary and respectful.

"Would you like to try?" she asked me, lifting a skewer of pork off a banana leaf from her cart. Still too frightened to try meat from a street food vendor, I shook my head no with deep sorrow and walked on.

I spotted a quaint restaurant with a patio perfect for solo dining about five blocks away from my apartment. Sitting down alone for dinner at first felt a little odd, but soon I was greeted with a friendly bow from the restaurant owner. After he placed a menu filled with photos of mouthwatering dishes in front of me, I quickly forgot my self-consciousness and ordered a personal feast.

A few minutes later, a large platter was set down in front of me. Heaping piles of orange, buttery chicken sat in a spicy coconut curry broth on the plate in front of me, releasing a heavenly aroma into the air. Scooping steaming piles of white rice into the coconut concoction, I cried a few tears of joy. I topped the meal off with a homemade fruit smoothie and mango sticky rice for dessert. Afterward, slipping into a food coma as jet lag began to truly sink in, I slowly found the way back to my gorgeous solo apartment, lay back down on my glorious king bed, and closed my eyes for a quick nap.

I woke up to my phone ringing. It was Sean, calling to let me know his flight had landed. Sean worked with me in Minnesota; we were both residents in the same internal medicine residency program. He had been selected as the second resident from our program to work in Thailand for the month of January. This had made me nervous at first. Although I knew Sean as a professional acquaintance in Minnesota, we were not friends.

Sean and I had worked together for six short weeks in Minnesota prior to our time in Chiang Mai. In those six weeks, I had learned that he was smart, hardworking, and motivated. Despite six weeks of sharing an office and a list of patients, however, Sean and I had not grown close or friendly. I actually got the impression that he was not interested in friendship because his professional personality was intense and all encompassing.

One month before our departure, I'd run into Sean at the hospital and had seen him reading a Buddhist philosophical book. He'd looked up at me with kind eyes and asked, "Would you be interested in joining me for a meditation retreat while we're in Thailand?"

Shocked, I'd felt my fear evaporate and found myself making plans with him. "Absolutely. I've also been looking at booking a tour at an ethical elephant sanctuary. Would you like to join?" Sean and I found common ground and shared excitement before we departed for Thailand. I looked forward to spending more time getting to know him, figuring when two people travel across the world together, it's a decently good opportunity to become fast friends.

Now we were here, in Thailand, and Sean said he was ready for dinner. Feeling like an expert on Chiang Mai after my half-mile walk to and from the restaurant, I offered to show him around.

I met Sean at an adorable outdoor café for my second dinner, at a table blanketed by a soft, copper-hued glow from string lights hanging overhead. We ordered Burmese-style pork curry, a northern Thai delicacy inspired by dishes from neighboring Myanmar (formerly Burma). This pork was melt-in-your-mouth good, the best I have ever tasted. I still salivate as I remember the glaze, a subtle sweetness of pineapple under a sauce of curried heat.

The two of us sat under the lights and talked for hours. There was no predicted awkwardness, no professionalism. After dinner, Sean asked, "Do you think we should grab another drink at the bar down the street?"

Smiling under the romantic glow of string lights overhead, I nodded. "Yes, I think we should."

We walked down Nimmanhaemin Road together, dodging raving motorbikes and herds of tourists. As we sat at yet another beautiful table under soft lights, Sean told me about his girlfriend home in Minnesota.

So this will not be a love story after all, I sadly thought to myself as I hugged him goodbye and headed home.

4

Following the Monk's Trail to enlightenment

Things are always changing, changing, changing.

—the Dalai Lama

Waking up alone to the sound of birds chirping, wrapped in a fluffy, luxurious white duvet, I smiled and hopped out of bed to practice yoga in my sun-drenched living room. Remembering our conversation from the previous night, I found myself somewhat relieved to recall that Sean was not single as I had assumed he was. I was in Thailand, having an incredible opportunity of cultural and spiritual exploration, and I did not need a man to complicate things. At least, that's what I told myself.

After an hour with my eyes glued to a Thailand tourist book, I called my new friend Sean. "How would you feel about an adventurous hike to a magical temple today?"

The little-known, extremely challenging Monk's Trail winds up Doi Suthep mountain to a majestic, golden temple called Wat Phra That Doi Suthep, the same temple that I could see shining from the mountain behind my apartment every time I stepped onto my balcony. Sean and I, both seriously into fitness, felt our bodies could use a tough hike after the two days we'd spent sitting on planes. He met me outside my apartment complex in athletic gear, sweat already dripping down our foreheads as we stood in the sweltering morning heat.

Most tourists grab a ride from downtown Chiang Mai to the top of Doi Suthep on a songthaew, a bright red open-air truck used as a shared taxi service you can find packed with locals and tourists alike. Hikers who attempt the full journey, however, are greatly rewarded. Midway up the mountain, a second, lesser-known temple, Wat Pha Lat, sits undisturbed in the forest, away from the paved roads the songthaews must take. Promises of an elusive, hidden temple intrigued us enough to attempt the full journey.

"How do we get to the Monk's Trail?" Sean asked.

I chuckled and quietly told him, "Well, we have to walk three miles through downtown Chiang Mai to get to the trail."

Looking at the ground, expecting Sean to think I was nuts, I heard him say, "This sounds awesome. Let's go!"

I remember feeling exhilarated as we strolled past a mix of charming cafés, street-food vendors, stray dogs, gorgeous gardens, and red songthaews overflowing with passengers, all the while trying not to misstep off the narrow, cracked tightrope of a sidewalk onto the street, where motorbikes raced past us at seventy miles per hour. A few miles into our walk, the scenery changed from bustling urban street to peaceful, winding road, leading us past local farms and neighborhoods. The humidity blanketed us, and the sun turned our pale winter noses bright red.

A mile or two down the quiet road, a large temple appeared. "We haven't even made it to the Monk's Trail yet," I told Sean, confused about the structure in front of us. We soon concluded that this was just a humble neighborhood temple. This structure whose architecture would be seen as something out of a stunning, magical dream in any city in the United States was not even listed on the map here. This was simply one of many temples, not the one the Monk's Trail promised to lead us to.

Regardless, this was my first glimpse of a temple in Thailand, and I was mesmerized. I begged Sean to take a half-mile detour down the gravel driveway to the unexpected sight.

"Let's check it out," he agreed. We veered right, stopping to take pictures and giving each other occasional looks of awe and amazement. Farther down the driveway, we were suddenly greeted by three unhappy and territorial stray dogs.

I love dogs—my dog at home is my sweet furry child whom I would do anything for—yet these dogs absolutely terrified me. They were angry, hungry, and bared their teeth as they ran toward us. Sean and I quickly remembered we didn't have cell phone service or any medical supplies with us. We also realized if these dogs bit us, our nearest rabies booster was over two hours away in Bangkok. I looked at Sean, terrified. "Let's back away as slowly as we can," he suggested.

My mind was telling me *Run fast as if your life depends on it,* but I knew Sean was right. Never turning our backs, we walked slowly and peacefully away until we reached the main road, the dogs staring us down the entire time.

Hearts thumping, sweat dripping, Sean and I looked at each other and hugged, letting out an enormous sigh. "That was really fucking close," I nervously said, giggling as my heart continued to race.

Fear is an interesting emotion. I can probably count in single digits the number of times I have experienced truly heart-racing, profound fear—it is thankfully not a common occurrence. Why do we feel fear? Evolutionarily, we are hardwired for our sympathetic nervous system, or our fight-or-flight response, to kick into overdrive when we encounter a dangerous situation. This is beneficial for the preservation of our species.

Yet, on a more personal note, the times I can vividly recall fear in my own life have little to do with situations requiring me to fight or flee from an animal predator. This one was a first. Others are less cinematic, less vivid, yet equally frightening:

I remember the intense fear I had as I told a patient for the first time that he was dying. His wife and daughter sat by his side holding his hand, my own hand pressing a stack of towels over the profusely bleeding wound in his abdomen.

I remember the fear of loss I felt the first time a man I was in love with cheated on me, kissing another girl behind the high school.

I remember hearing about an army helicopter pilot killed in a crash the first time my brother was deployed with the military. I was overcome by a premature fear that my brother could be on the news someday as well.

I remember the day I decided to leave my husband—the fear I felt of breaking his heart and his family's hearts, of breaking societal norms, of starting over without any guarantee for romantic happiness.

I remember the first time I led a "code blue," an emergency medical response where I stood at the bed of a patient who had lost her heartbeat and directed a team of twenty nurses, students, and support staff as they tried to resuscitate her. I remember fear as I picked up the phone to call her husband when she did not survive.

These moments of fear are vivid in my memory, and it's unlikely I'll ever forget them. Fear, in my opinion, can teach us valuable lessons. When we think back to the few times we have felt true fear, why did we feel it? Did it help us? Did it hurt us? Perhaps it did neither. Perhaps for you, as it did for me, fear simply burned into your brain the concrete seal of a memory that nothing can shake. Fear reminded me that I am not invincible. Fear reminded me that stability is an illusion, that everything is impermanent. Fear forced me to be malleable and to accept that human life will have suffering, despite all our plans to avoid it.

Once the danger is behind us, once the fear has decreased and we regain our footing on solid ground, we may experience one of life's greatest feelings: absolute peace. As I type this, thinking about these fear-inducing moments of my short life, my heart starts to race. Yet, as I remember that these moments are no longer active or threatening, I find myself breathing out deeply, tearing up, and feeling pure gratefulness to be free of those fearful situations. The escape from the thing that scares us, once freedom and safety are regained, may bring a sense of peace nearly nothing else can.

On our way to the Monk's Trail, my experience with Sean made me remember this. A mile or so later, we made it to the end of the paved road and found a discreet, faded green sign. This sign said something in Thai we assumed to be "Welcome to the Monk's Trail." We could have been very wrong, but it looked promising.

Armed with nothing but a camera and a vague sense of where we were in the world, I realized a map, a bottle of water, or a shred of common sense might have been helpful had we brought them. The first few miles up the trail took us through dense vegetation. I could hear the musical trickling of small waterfalls and the soft ruffle of green leaves dancing above me. Apart from two runners who flew by in a frenzy, a child on his father's back, and a honeymooning couple holding hands, the trail was deserted.

"What are those?" Sean asked, pointing to faded, saffron-colored fabric ribbons tied around trees along the edge of the trail.

"Oh, I read about these," I confidently told him. "These ribbons were once tied around the waists of monks' robes. Many monks hike this trail in nothing but robes and sandals to get to Wat Phra That at the top. Isn't that incredible?"

We followed the trail outlined by the monks' fabric markers. Although at the time I thought these faded pieces of cloth were simply leading me to a gorgeous temple, I realize now that they led me on the start of an unbelievable journey, filled with exploration of culture, medicine, religion, health, spirituality, and love. I have no doubt that the noble monks on this trail before me led me to absolutely the correct place—in this world, and in this life.

Winding up the mountain deeper into the forest, I felt myself relax with each step. Within a clearing in the trees, an absolutely gorgeous temple emerged. Before it lay a trail of crumbling stone steps lined by decaying Buddhist sculptures on either side. "Sean, I think this is Wat Pha Lat," I said, smiling.

"It's incredible," Sean replied.

Temples in Thailand are not a single structure as you might picture them. Rather, temples are actually large outdoor areas with multiple separate buildings or covered structures used for silent prayer and meditation, with gardens and peaceful trails between structures. This particular temple was spread out over the equivalent of three city blocks, perched on top of a flowing waterfall. As we hiked the crumbling stone steps, we passed a silent meditation hut on our left and a waterfall on our right. The mouth of the waterfall was surrounded by two giant stone dragon heads which welcomed visitors up a second, enormous stone staircase to a collection of colorful buildings on the hill above.

The scene was breathtaking. To this day, I can close my eyes and see Wat Pha Lat. Sometimes, I think I may have dreamt the entire scene.

Sean and I found a small open-air structure available for quiet meditation. We sat with eyes closed, legs crossed. While I had never meditated outdoors before, I found myself surprisingly relaxed. I let my thoughts flow over me like passing clouds, coming and going, impermanent in nature. I thanked the world and the Buddha for this moment of joy.

Afterward, continuing up the staircase, my eyes found one incredible piece of art after another: golden sculptures of Buddha, mosaic-tiled elephants, and enormous marble dragons. Art that could inspire awe in any luxurious museum anywhere in the world was sitting outside, in the open air, in the middle of a forest in Thailand halfway up a mountain. "I never want to leave," I told Sean, yet our journey was nowhere near complete.

After soaking in the magic of Wat Pha Lat, we continued on the trail toward Wat Phra That Doi Suthep, our highly anticipated destination. Ancient Buddhist wisdom says that a Buddha relic, a piece of bone, once broke in two pieces. One piece is located at Wat Suan Dok, a temple located in central Chiang Mai. The other piece of bone was placed on a great white elephant who carried it up the mountain of Doi Suthep. Where the elephant stopped, and supposedly died, is where the other piece of bone was left and the Wat Phra That temple was built.

The journey on this second segment of the trail was incredibly challenging, consisting of steep, narrow trails without an end in sight. The humidity made my breathing shallow. Despite a year of working on my physical endurance through challenging daily exercise, I felt out of shape.

A few miles of elevation later, we saw bright saffron robes hanging out to dry on balconies ahead. Following a group of young teenage monks to the opening of the Wat Phra That temple, we stood silently in awe.

In front of us stood an enormous structure, whose central building was topped with a large chedi fully covered in gold. Thousands of monks in saffron robes carried flowers and incense into the temple. We took off our shoes as a sign of respect, walked slowly into the temple, and knelt in front of a golden Buddha. I closed my eyes and thought to myself: *Enjoy every little moment; for these are often life's greatest moments passing us by.*

5

Work begins

*If you think you are too small to make a
difference, try sleeping with a mosquito.*

—the Dalai Lama

A few days later, I started my medical rotation in Thailand. I had
initially planned to spend my month working in the Thai traditional and complementary medicine clinic to learn the ancient art
of Thai massage and acupuncture; however, this clinic was closed
the first week of my visit. I was reassigned, quite ironically, to work
on the oncology service which specialized in cancers of various
natures, including the brain.

Sean called me the morning work began to let me know that
he too had been assigned to the oncology service. "Should we walk
together?" he asked kindly. A few moments later, I found myself
standing outside Sean's apartment, where he waited for me with a
cappuccino in hand.

One wrong turn led to another, and by the time we finally saw
the hospital ahead we were running quite late. Entering the first
open door we saw, we suddenly smelled the familiar and disgusting odor of formaldehyde. Peering to our right, we saw the un-
mistakable smell was coming from a room where white body bags
lined the tables and dissection tools hung overhead. "Remember
anatomy class?" I asked Sean.

"Of course," he replied, "that's a smell and an experience that
can never be forgotten."

Any physician you talk to will remember the experience of his or her first anatomy class. For some horrifically morbid reason, the smell of formaldehyde mixed with flesh makes you instinctually hungry. It is a terrible feeling to be hungry, often craving meat, while you are hands-deep in an open corpse.

My first corpse was a woman I named Susan. Many students name their corpses to make the experience more respectful and humbling. Susan was around seventy years old and had died from a massive aortic aneurysm rupture, which I quickly learned when I opened up her chest. She taught me and four of my medical school colleagues valuable lessons about anatomy, sacrifice, and the unbelievable reality that once we are dead, our bodies mean nothing to us whatsoever.

Shortly after my first anatomy class, one of my fellow medical students who had dissected Susan with me left the program. I learned six months later that she herself had died of metastatic breast cancer. For years, I was haunted to think that my classmate likely knew she was dying as she carved open Susan's body in order to teach herself how to help other patients. She didn't live long enough to graduate from medical school, but she was the best damn doctor I've ever met. There are so many people in this world stronger than you could ever realize.

Pulling myself out of my anatomical memories, I heard Sean say, "We're five minutes late already. Let's follow the group of physicians up ahead." We managed to find our way to the oncology clinic, arriving ten minutes late with sweat stains under our arms; the hospital was swelteringly hot and had no central air conditioning. An oncologist introduced himself and told me I could spend the day observing him work. After a quick goodbye, Sean was pulled into the clinic next door.

The oncology clinic was unlike anything I had ever seen in the United States. There were at least one hundred patients in the waiting room, piles of paper medical records on every desk, and very few computers in sight. The clinic room I sat in was the size of a large walk-in closet and held around eight people at a time (me, the oncologist, a second oncologist, the two patients these oncologists were seeing, plus any family members the patients brought with them). Patient privacy was minimal: with two physicians sharing one clinic room, everyone in the room could overhear each patient's story in surprisingly clear detail.

The oncologist pulled up a chair for me to sit at the desk next to him. Trying to keep fear out of my voice, I asked, "How many patients do you see in a given day?" The waiting room seemed to be at capacity.

"All the patients that need me," he replied matter-of-factly.

As patient after patient sat in front of us, the oncologist interpreted everything for me in English. Despite the utter chaos of his day, he crafted detailed, thoughtful diagnoses and treatment plans in rapid time.

On my first day, I met a sixty-year-old woman with newly diagnosed acute myeloid leukemia. She walked into the clinic smiling, and brought me and the oncologist a bag of cookies. I thanked her quietly in Thai and bowed in prayer. The oncologist told me it is not uncommon for patients to bring physicians small gifts in Thailand, although this is relatively uncommon in the United States. This patient had noticed me sitting next to her oncologist before her appointment, rushed to the hospital gift shop, and bought a second bag of cookies just for me. To this day, I am still touched by her kindness. This woman, entering what was likely one of the most stressful clinic appointments of her life, took moments of her precious day to get me a gift. I did not feel that I deserved that gift.

Next, I met a twenty-five-year-old man with a new diagnosis of diffuse large B-cell lymphoma. He was accompanied to the clinic by his young wife. I could see he was trying to hold back tears throughout the visit as his wife smiled and took detailed notes about the oncologist's recommendation to start urgent treatment. We brought this young man directly to the hospital to spend the night and start immediate intravenous chemotherapy. I ended up seeing him on hospital rounds the following day, his young, tired wife at his bedside. To my surprise, the couple recognized me immediately and smiled. I did not feel that I deserved that smile.

Later that afternoon, I met a fifty-year-old female nurse with a new diagnosis of late-stage chronic myeloid leukemia. She also brought me cookies. She also smiled. She cracked jokes and laughed as we talked about her life expectancy of mere months. I did not feel I deserved her cookies, her smile, or her laughter.

6

The net of gems

Everything in the universe is interconnected.
Within each it is reflected.

—Lourdes Pita

After a fascinating morning in clinic, I was given the afternoon off to explore town and settle in. I walked back to my apartment and spent a little time reading *The Universe in a Single Atom.* I underlined a giant passage during that reading session.

> In the Buddhist world, there is an acknowledgment of the practical impossibility of gaining total knowledge of the origin of the universe. A Mahayana text entitled *The Flower Ornament Scripture* contains a lengthy discussion of infinite world systems and the limits of human knowledge. A section called "The Incalculable" provides a string of calculations of extremely high numbers, culminating in terms such as "the incalculable," "the measureless," "the boundless," and "the incomparable." The highest number is the "square untold," which is said to be the function of the "unspeakable" multiplied by itself! [As an aside, I am a total math nerd and love this weird passage.] A friend told me that this number can be written as 10^{59}. The *Flower Ornament* goes on to apply these mind-boggling numbers to the universe systems; it suggests that if "untold" worlds are reduced to atoms and each atom contains "untold"

worlds, still the numbers of world systems will not be exhausted.

This concept left me speechless. At first I was profoundly confused, but then I started to think about the perpetuity of our universe. Buddhists reject the idea of the independent self. Instead, we acknowledge the profound interdependence of all beings. We are all connected. We depend on others for every single thing we do, and what we do has an effect on all those we interact with in our lifetime, even many we *don't* directly interact with.

The Dalai Lama compares the intricate and profoundly interconnected reality of the world to an infinite net of gems called "Indra's jeweled net," which reaches out to infinite space. Picture a net with a sparkling crystal gem upon every knot. Each bit of net connects to a crystal gem, and each gem shines a reflection onto itself and all the other gems in the infinitely larger net. On an infinite net, no crystal sits on the edge. If the universe is one enormous net of crystal gems with no true center and no edge, then every crystal will reflect back onto every other crystal forever, in all directions.

After I read this concept, I immediately loved it despite my profound confusion. When I think about it, I imagine a net filled with mirrored gems reflecting back on all the other gems, almost like a funhouse mirror that lets you visualize yourself in infinite repetitions.

I made Sean read this passage and spent the next many days referring to everything I could as the "net of gems." When something was surprising, interesting, or amazing, I made a "net of gems" joke. Sean laughed every time.

Later on, when I was diagnosed with a brain tumor, I couldn't help but wonder, *Did the stupid net finally break?*

It took me a while to realize that it did not. The net is intact. I am a gem on the net. You are a gem on the net. Everything about you and everything about this universe is a gem. The net will never break. Infinite possibilities await us all. Trust that the net will be there to catch you even when you fall from a frightening height.

7

Are you happy?

*There is an inextricable link between one's personal
happiness and kindness, compassion, and caring
for others. And this is a two-way street: increased
happiness leads to greater compassion, and increased
compassion leads to greater happiness.*

—the Dalai Lama

After a week on the oncology service, my first weekend in Thailand arrived. One of my dreams had always been to meet an elephant. After extensive research into ethical elephant experiences, I found a sanctuary that did not allow elephant riding and instead offered a unique, personalized full-day hike through the jungle with opportunities to meet and feed elephants along the way. "Sean, do you want to spend a day with elephants?" I asked, knowing full well his answer would be, "Absolutely."

An open-air truck arrived to pick us up bright and early on Saturday morning. Sean and I hopped in the back, hands tightly gripping the rusted seats as the rickety truck sped down miles of rough highway. An hour later, we reached a narrow gravel road and parked outside a small, secluded elephant eco-lodge nestled in the northern Thai jungle. Stepping off the truck, I could see smiling elephants in the forest all around me. I had never felt such pure, unadulterated joy as I did the first time I saw an elephant smile.

The elephants were not on chains. They were roaming around the sanctuary, eating bananas and bathing themselves in the river.

Female elephants with their babies picked up mud with their long trunks and tossed it hilariously up onto their backs, a technique they use to keep themselves cool and protect themselves from the sun.

These magnificent, wise creatures were the most beautiful things I had ever seen. The elephants often walked up to me, smelled me, and gave me looks of concern. One female followed me around all morning, often holding her trunk up to the right side of my head and sniffing me. Giggling at the tickle the tiny hairs on the end of her trunk created, I didn't even consider that she may have been trying to tell me something I was not yet ready to hear.

Following the jungle hike, our adventure continued with a river rafting experience. Sean and I were ushered onto a narrow bamboo raft captained by a local Karen man, a member of the largest hill tribe group in northern Thailand. Our captain hummed soft songs as he steered our raft down a peaceful stream. With cool, clear water beneath and large, green leafy trees above, I felt profound peace.

Farther down the river, we came across a local Karen family sitting on a small, rickety patio next to the edge of the water. The mother smiled as her children waved at us with fervent excitement. I do not know how much English this woman spoke, but as our raft sailed by, she stood up without clear reason and asked me as loudly and proudly as she could in broken English, "Are you happy?"

My only thought was, *I've never been happier.*

8

What went wrong?

*Dear teacher, when I was a governor, my palace was
guarded by hundreds of soldiers. But I was still very
afraid. I was afraid robbers would come and kill me
or at least take away all my valuables . . . But last
night [after leaving his palace behind to become a
monk] I realized that now I have nothing to lose . . .
Nobody wants to kill me anymore because I have no
power, no wealth, and no jewels for anyone to take.
I have nothing. Yet, I finally have everything.*

—the story of Badhiya, a cousin of the
Buddha, as told by Thich Nhat Hanh

The following week, I transitioned from working in the oncology
clinic to working with the palliative care team. Here, I met Ms. A.
Ms. A was a palliative care nurse whom I would soon consider my
Thai mom. On our first day together, she looked at me with a huge
smile on her face and asked, "Do you like to shop?" We became
instant friends.

Ms. A invited me to shop with her at her favorite local market
in town after work. We hopped in a red songthaew and drove
to the market, located in Chiang Mai's Chinatown. The market
was enormous; it spanned at least twenty city blocks. This seemingly endless space was filled with amazing, locally made goods
handcrafted by hill tribe villagers. I tried on a stylish, exquisitely
tailored jacket and purchased it for an unbelievably cheap price.

I regret that I never got the chance to wear that jacket while in Thailand, as my trip soon took an unexpected detour.

Ms. A, along with many of my other Thai friends, was surprised to learn that I consider myself a Buddhist. "I'm so happy to hear this," she told me, grabbing my hand and cheerfully exclaiming, "We must see one of the city's oldest temples, it's just this way!" Following her lead, we entered a temple lined by golden dragons with a large golden Buddha inside. Ms. A taught me the appropriate way to bow and pay respect to the Buddha—never point your feet directly at the Buddha's representation, never take a photograph inside the temple, and always give an offering (flower, money, incense, love) to the Buddha and the Sangha (Buddhist community) before you leave.

For dinner, Ms. A brought me to a hilarious, tiny "American country-western"–themed restaurant nearby for a family-style feast. During dinner, she asked, "How old are you? You look so young, so pretty."

Blushing, I said, "I'm only twenty-nine. But I've already been married and divorced, so I feel a million years older."

Ms. A's mouth dropped open, "You're divorced? How is this possible? What silly man would leave a sweet, pretty woman like you?" Leaning forward, she confided, "I'm fifty-three. I'm still single, but I'm looking for a man." She grabbed my hands from across the table and looked into my eyes. "There is a man out there for us. We can't give up hope."

I giggled hysterically and smiled at this wonderful, kind woman across from me. Still stunned that she was in her early fifties, I asked her, "How do you look so young? What's your secret?"

Without any hesitation, Ms. A giggled in turn and said, "I EAT!" So eat we did.

After a few days on the palliative care service, I was finally scheduled to start work in the Thai traditional and complementary medicine clinic the next day. Although I would miss Ms. A, I was looking forward to learning some Eastern medical techniques I hoped could supplement my Western medical knowledge.

I woke up the following morning feeling like I was coming down with a cold. Dismayed, I took some ibuprofen, threw on a mask, and decided to walk the thirty minutes into clinic despite my symptoms since this type of medical and cultural educational experience doesn't come along every day. Physicians often make terrible patients themselves.

My cold-like symptoms improved with my walk into clinic. It was a beautiful, sunny day as usual in Chiang Mai. Arriving at the clinic, I was quickly ushered into the Chinese medicine department, where a physician asked if I would be interested in trying acupuncture myself to learn what it was like. I happily agreed, having never tried this before. As I lay on the table, face down, needles covering my back and neck, I started to feel extremely feverish. I had severe chills, the kind that make your whole body shake and your teeth rattle. I felt so miserable, I had to call the doctor back in to remove the needles early. I'm not a quitter, and this felt like quitting. Angry at myself and my body for failing me, I reluctantly decided to take the afternoon off. I hopped into a songthaew to take me home and crawled into bed.

After I arrived home, the fever intensified. I didn't have a thermometer in Thailand, so this personal case report is sadly lacking in quantitative data. However, I recall vividly that I alternated between sweating profusely and shaking with chills.

During one episode of these rigors, I was lying in bed and felt my left-hand muscles contracting rapidly. This was odd, and I couldn't explain it at the time. I drank some water, took another ibuprofen, and napped for the rest of the afternoon.

I woke up that evening feeling better. Sean called and offered, "Let me bring you some dinner."

"I'm feeling a bit better; do you think we could find some soup?" I asked. Sean knocked on my door ten minutes later, and we walked to a local restaurant that served delicious warm rice noodles in a curried chicken broth. I slurped down every bite and hoped by morning I'd feel good as new.

Unfortunately, the following morning I woke up drenched in sweat. My fever had returned. I had never taken a sick day from work in my life, but I was so uncomfortably ill that I asked my clinic director for the day off. I slept in until noon, popped a few ibuprofens, and rejoiced as I felt my fever subside. Although I likely should have stayed home, I decided to venture out and explore.

I figured an authentic Thai massage might be good for me. A nearby spa offered a three-hour experience, complete with Thai massage, oil massage, and a facial. The masseuse stretched me into deeply painful but intensely wonderful positions for the first hour of the session. This was followed by a sixty-minute oil massage, similar to a Western Swedish massage; the experience was topped off with an hour-long facial, during which I fell into the deepest, most pleasant sleep of my life. I was awoken to a facial treatment where a putty the consistency of mud and honey was slapped onto my face until my skin was smooth as a newborn's. Finished, I was treated to a hot tea and a cookie to finish the entire three-hour experience.

The following day was a good one. I woke up feeling healthy and rested, then spent the day working in clinic. I also found a local yoga studio holding a relaxing yoga flow class that evening. As I entered the yoga studio and started class, I was surprised and pleased to find that yoga is a somewhat universal language. The flow was very similar to yoga at home.

A very cute yogi who looked to be in his mid-thirties and had a fascinating tattoo on his muscular shoulder was next to me in class. As we were leaving, he introduced himself to me. "Hey, I'm Max."

Blushing, I softly responded, "I'm Courtney. Where are you from?" Max was from New York. He was living in Thailand for a few months, working remotely. He invited me to dinner later that evening, and I raced home to get ready for what would be my first real date since my marital separation.

Dressed in a silky black top and a patterned skirt, I walked a mile through the busy streets of downtown Chiang Mai, nervously wondering if I would remember how to have a conversation with Max once I arrived. I saw the sign for Kao Soy Nimman, my favorite spot in the city, one block in front of me. The sign's orange glow welcomed visitors onto a large outdoor dining area. I could see Max sitting at a table on the patio, waiting for me.

Suddenly, I felt an intense sensation of cramping in my left hand. This cramping was brief, maybe twenty seconds, but it was followed by a strong sensation of dysphagia, or an inability to swallow. As I looked longingly at Kao Soy Nimman, Max at a table merely feet in front of me, I had to stop. I took a step backward, hiding my face from the orange glow as I felt the muscles of my throat spasm intensely, making it impossible for me to swallow my own saliva. I remember feeling saliva pool in the left side of my mouth and start to drool down my face. This was terrifying and disgusting, but brief. Within ten seconds, it stopped. I cleared my throat, regained control of myself, and thought about what had just happened. I was awake, conscious, and walking the entire time. *What the hell?*

I had no idea what I had just experienced, but I chalked it up to a strange episode of anxiety before the date. Feeling nervous but otherwise fine, I walked into the restaurant and enjoyed a spicy coconut curry khao soi dish and a nice conversation with Max. My anxiety eased up the longer I sat with him, and I had nearly forgotten about the muscle cramping episode by the time I left the restaurant a few hours later.

I walked home and curled into bed, thinking of the exciting weekend I would soon spend with elephants. After my first elephant adventure, I had immediately booked myself a second, solo two-day elephant experience at another ethical elephant sanctuary called the Elephant Nature Park. ENP is a fabulous ethical sanctuary and rescue center for elephants, dogs, and cats founded by Lek Chailert in the 1990s. Its mission is to provide a home for endangered animals as well as contribute to the welfare and development of these beautiful creatures. It offers a unique opportunity for visitors to volunteer at the sanctuary and learn how to feed and care for elephants.

A small van picked me up from my apartment and brought me to ENP, about an hour north of Chiang Mai, for the weekend. I had the most amazing, incredible, life-changing weekend there. I fell completely in love with the magical giants around me. They made me feel more joy than I had felt in a very long time. I was symptom-free, without any scary muscle-cramping events, and helped care for rescued elephants all weekend long. I returned to Chiang Mai on Sunday evening, feeling physically exhausted but mentally refreshed.

I spent Sunday evening sitting in bed back in my apartment, researching my next two travel adventures. After much consideration, I decided the first would be a solo hiking trip to Colombia in April, the second an island-hopping adventure in Greece in July. I was saving my well-researched itineraries in my type-A travel planning folder on my computer when suddenly, an all-too-familiar sensation of left-hand cramping began. As I had come to expect, the throat-tightening and inability to swallow came next. The episode was brief, thirty seconds at most, but this time I did not have pre-date anxiety to explain my symptoms. I fell asleep, trying to forget anything strange had happened.

I woke up the next day, went to work, and walked to a small local market on the way home to find a few souvenirs for my family. As I stood outside the open-air market, I felt the same awful muscle cramping start again, out of nowhere.

I stepped out of the tent I was in and hid myself between two vendor stalls as I prepared for what I knew was coming next. My left-hand muscles contracted rapidly, squeezing my fingers together as if I had no control over them. A few seconds later, hand now relaxed, my throat closed up on me. This time, the saliva pooled more rapidly than before, and I felt a small drop of drool drip onto my left shoulder. *Seriously, what the hell?* I was scared. Once again, a mere thirty seconds later, my muscles relaxed and all was back to normal.

I tried to medically rationalize the random, temporary muscle cramping I had experienced. In my mind, I thought, *This could be an electrolyte imbalance, dehydration, infection, or simply anxiety. Oh god, I guess it could be a partial seizure as well, but why? No, a pseudo-seizure, an anxiety-provoked neurological event, is much more likely.* As an otherwise healthy twenty-nine-year-old female with no other symptoms and no reason for a seizure, I tried to brush this off and decided I would worry more if it happened again.

I would soon determine that these were in fact focal seizures, my body's one and only symptom of brain cancer. Literally one week prior to this, I'd had no symptoms of the golf ball–sized tumor growing in my skull—no headaches, no nausea, no vomiting, no speech or balance issues, no weight loss. I wasn't even tired. I felt amazing, actually! I was in the best shape of my life.

Feeling a bit better the following day, I decided to resume my yoga practice, so I packed my travel mat and walked over to the studio for an early evening vinyasa flow. This class was challenging and included headstand practice. I looked around for Max, but he wasn't in class that day. We had dinner plans for the following weekend.

I put my head on the floor in front of me and effortlessly lifted my legs above me, again finding this position as natural as walking. Class ended, so I packed up my mat, put on my shoes, and began my walk home. No more than one block later, I suddenly experienced the cramping all over again. I continued to walk, shaking my left hand in front of me as if I could shake away the muscle spasms. Twenty seconds or so later, the hand cramping ended just in time for me to feel my throat muscles start to constrict. I tried not to panic. At that moment, I was walking in front of a 7-Eleven convenience store on the busiest street in Chiang Mai. I stood on the front steps of this 7-Eleven and attempted to take a drink from my water bottle, thinking if this was anxiety or insanity, perhaps I could distract myself long enough for the symptoms to end.

A cool sip of water hit my tongue and proceeded to fall slowly out of the left corner of my mouth. Realizing I was literally unable to swallow, I started to panic. I put my water bottle away. I looked around and saw nervous faces staring back at me, watching a strange foreign girl on the steps of a 7-Eleven with panic in her eyes and drool coming out of her mouth.

Ashamed, I looked at the ground, took a deep breath, and waited for the symptoms to subside. Thirty seconds later, as I had expected, I felt normal. I took out my bottle once again and gulped down a successful drink of water. I walked four blocks home, embarrassed, terrified, and aware that I could no longer ignore the symptoms my body was repeatedly giving me. I never went back to that 7-Eleven.

Arriving home, I switched roles from scared solo traveler to internal medicine physician and tried to come up with a logical diagnosis. I thought through my list of symptoms, the pattern of occurrence, the rapid self-resolution, and the various triggers (fever, anxiety, yoga headstand).

I made a differential diagnosis for myself. In medicine, a differential diagnosis is a list of possible diagnoses that fit with a patient's variety of symptoms, akin to a detective identifying a list of suspects, ready to rule them out one by one.

The differential diagnosis list I created for myself included various possibilities. The simplest, least terrifying option was muscle cramping due to dehydration or electrolyte imbalance in the setting of recent viral illness and overexertion. Medically, however,

I knew this did not quite fit. Muscle cramping isolated to two very specific areas would be unusual. Next on my list was pseudo-seizure, a psychosomatic seizure-like event often triggered subconsciously by anxiety or other mental illness. I hoped this was the answer, but also found it strange that my body would display anxiety in such an extremely physical way when I wasn't feeling any extreme anxiety mentally.

Infection was next on my list. I had spent the two previous weekends with elephants, surrounded by tropical jungles, sleeping under old mosquito netting. Perhaps I had caught a strange neurologic infection such as Japanese encephalitis. This would be terrible. An incurable neurologic infectious disease? No, I didn't want my mind to go there.

Focal or partial seizure was last on my list. I willed seizure not to be on the list, but the symptoms fit. Time-limited, specific patterns of inexplicable and unplanned sensations occurring in a repetitive pattern after various triggers? A detective would have said, "*I've cracked the case.*"

But why? I wondered. I was a healthy young woman without any history of seizures. I did not have epilepsy, I had been drinking very little alcohol, and I had not recently started any new medications that could trigger a seizure. It didn't make any sense. Despite this, I knew as a physician that if a patient told me about these symptoms, I would reach out to a colleague in neurology to inquire about possible seizures.

I called one of my best friends back home, Stephanie, and asked her to discuss my case with a neurology resident. She tried to reassure me, saying, "These probably aren't seizures, but I'll ask a neurologist I'm working with."

After I spent an hour waiting anxiously by the phone, she called back. "I told the neurologist about your case. He agreed with you, there is a small chance these could be focal seizures. He recommended you get a medical workup as soon as possible."

"Well, shit," I told her. "Thanks. I'll call you later."

At this point, it was late in the evening in Thailand. The emergency medical system works differently there, and I was not at all excited about the prospect of spending the rest of the night sitting in an emergency triage center without the ability to effectively describe my symptoms in the Thai language. Instead, I called my emergency contact at Chiang Mai University, one of the physicians I had worked with at the palliative care clinic. Very fortunately, this physician also happened to be a board-certified neurologist. To this day I thank my lucky stars for Dr. Pertha.*

I described my symptoms to Dr. Pertha on the phone late that evening. I felt like a fool, bothering her at night for what was likely nothing to worry about. I tried to explain my symptoms as a physician would, consulting another physician on an unusual case. This strategy worked. Dr. Pertha agreed with me and told me to meet her the following morning and walk with her to the neurology clinic.

Lying in bed that night, I had another cramping event, exactly the same as before. I knew then, without a doubt, that these were focal seizures. I needed help.

---

* An asterisk throughout this book denotes a name I have changed to protect the privacy of physicians and patients.

9

The diagnosis

We are born with the seed of our own death. From the moment of birth, we are approaching this inevitable demise. Then we must also contemplate that the time of our death is uncertain. Death does not wait for us to tidy up our lives. It strikes unannounced.

—the Dalai Lama

Waking up, I was filled with anxiety but felt fine physically. I walked two miles to the hospital to meet Dr. Pertha, who then accompanied me to the neurology clinic.

The neurology clinic looked eerily similar to the oncology clinic I'd worked in the previous week. The waiting room was filled with hundreds of people, all speaking quickly in Thai as they waited for their appointments. Dr. Pertha spoke to the receptionist and told me to wait until my name was called. After reassuring me that the neurologist spoke some English, she left me in the waiting room and headed back to her own clinic.

I sat alone in the busy waiting room, looking around to see dozens of eyes staring directly at me, the lone foreigner in the middle of the room. While waiting, I planned out the story I would tell the neurologist. If this clinic worked in a similar way to the oncology clinic, I knew I would have somewhere between two to five minutes to explain my symptoms and convince the physician that they were real and not the anxious manifestations of a young hypochondriac. I would then advocate to get an MRI scan of my brain.

An hour later, with sweaty palms and a voice shaking with nerves, my name was finally called. I walked into the clinic room, shared with a second patient and her physician, and introduced myself to the neurologist, Dr. Nera.* Here I was, both patient and physician for the first time in my life, unsure of my identity or how to act.

I told Dr. Nera my story. I told him I was also a physician. I said I knew these symptoms could be a figment of an anxious imagination, but I was confident that I had enough signs pointing to focal seizures that I required an urgent MRI. The neurologist looked quizzically at me, not quite sure what to make of a young, bossy American physician-patient sitting in front of him diagnosing herself with seizures and requesting a specific workup. I thought, *I must sound crazy. I am crazy.*

The neurologist had me do a brief neurological exam, an exam I was quite familiar with myself. As the test progressed, his expression changed. We realized together that my left hand displayed slight weakness compared with my right hand. My shocked eyes looked into his. "I agree with an MRI," he said. "These could be pseudoseizures, but I don't know for sure."

Feeling both grateful and terrified, I was placed in a wheelchair and brought downstairs to the hospital entrance, where a nurse told me I would be transported to the nearby imaging center. Apparently, the MRI machine was not located within the hospital itself.

The transportation vehicle turned out to be an ancient ambulance, no longer used for emergencies, instead equipped with a few torn seats and outdated medical supplies. I was ushered into the back of this vehicle along with four other patients and their families. No one spoke any English during the brief ride to the imaging center. I sat quietly, looking around at the frail, elderly patients in the ambulance with me, praying that none of them would have a true emergency on the way to the imaging center.

Fortunately, the four other patients were still alive and well by the time we parked at the imaging center. I checked in with the receptionist and waited an hour for my scan. During this hour, I grabbed *The Universe in a Single Atom* from my purse, tried to focus in on the Dalai Lama's words, and happened to finish the book shortly before my name was called.

"Courtney, we're ready for you," the receptionist said, motioning for me to follow a nurse into another room.

A nurse took me back to the MRI room, gave me a hospital gown to change into, and asked me to sign a financial agreement. In Thailand, medical payments work much differently than in the United States. Medical quotes are predetermined. Patients are asked to sign agreements before their procedure, test, or treatment begins. I signed a bill agreeing to pay 8,000 Thai bait, or at that time around US $250, for my MRI scan. I lay down on the table, stuffed like a sardine into a tiny, outdated machine.

Compared to MRI machines at home, this one was large, bulky, and frightening. I did not receive headphones playing relaxing classical music to lull me to sleep, nor was I offered anxiolytic medication to curb claustrophobia. Instead, the radiology technician played intense Thai-pop dance music and left the room.

Lying there in the MRI machine, I decided I must be losing my mind. "These must be panic attacks," I told myself, only to start feeling my left hand tingle and my throat muscles tighten as the threatening Thai-pop music seemed to grow louder with every breath.

I lay in the MRI scanner for forty-five minutes before the tech reentered the room. Expecting him to say I was finished, I was surprised when he instead asked me to sign a second financial agreement. In limited English, he asked, "Is it OK to charge you another 8,000 Thai bait for the surgical planning MRI now?"

"Excuse me, a surgical planning MRI? Sir, I am a physician," I said. "I assume this means you found something on the first scan if you need a surgical planning scan now?"

"Yes," he responded.

Keeping my questions brief due to our language barrier, I asked him, "How many masses did you see on the scan? One or multiple?"

"One mass," was all he said. I agreed to pay the money and spent the next and longest twenty minutes of my life creating an updated differential diagnosis in my mind.

Differential diagnoses for one brain mass leading to recurrent focal seizures. Brain abscess, a focal pocket of infection, was first on my list. I had spent days playing with so many beautiful but dirty elephants. At one point, I'd even hopped in the stream to bathe them. No doubt I had caught a parasitic infection that invaded my brain. *How could I have been so stupid and careless?* I thought.

Next on my list was a camera smudge. I was lying in an ancient MRI machine with fairly outdated computers around me—this must be simply a technical glitch and a big misunderstanding.

The inner patient in me didn't want to consider the last possibility on my differential diagnosis list, but the inner physician in me knew I must. A brain tumor. One mass, one life-changing realization.

As my scan ended, I realized the neurologist I'd met earlier that day had told me he would not have time to read my scan until the following morning. With a life-threatening brain infection on my differential, however, I knew this would not do.

I got off the MRI table and walked into the technologist's command center, feeling terrified yet confident that this moment called for the greatest bravery of my life. I told him, "As I mentioned, I am a physician. I need to see my scan results and take a few pictures." Being the only physician in the imaging center, the technologist reluctantly agreed and scrolled through the images on his computer.

On the screen in front of me, I saw an enormous, golf ball–sized, irregularly shaped mass in my right frontal lobe. The mass was huge, so large that it caused minor mass effect, a medical term which means the tumor was essentially smooshing healthy brain tissue toward the left side of my head as good and bad brain fought for the same space inside a finite skull space.

As I numbly snapped a few photos with my cell phone, I tried to process what I was seeing on the screen in front of me. My first thought was, *Well, shit, I'm going to have to tell this patient some bad news today. She has a massive brain tumor.*

Remembering the patient was myself, I went into a momentary shock.

The radiology tech said, "OK, that's enough time," and abruptly kicked me out of the room. "The radiologist will call you with the results tomorrow." Speechless, I left the clinic.

There I was, standing on the sidewalk in Chiang Mai, trying to process what I had just seen on my own scan. The physician in me knew this was either a tumor or, less likely, an abscess, both of which could be considered medical emergencies requiring prompt evaluation and treatment.

Why would a healthy, happy, thriving young physician have a brain tumor, I wondered. And what cruel world or deity would give her this diagnosis while she was about to start the last week of her lovely self-exploratory journey in Thailand?

Initially, I felt as though I were talking to the tumor directly. "Tumor, didn't you think to check with me first to make sure I was OK sharing this special part of my frontal lobe with you before you so selfishly took over my territory?" I asked. Stupid tumor didn't respond. "I don't feel comfortable with you in there, so close to me and my secret thoughts."

Honestly, I thought for a few minutes I could bargain with the tumor and leave it to cower in fear after seeing it had made a horrible mistake messing with the wrong, stubborn lady. Unfortunately, my uninvited guest knew that it held all the power between the two of us. At that moment, the tumor took over my life. In seconds, it took away every hope and dream I had ever had for myself. Terror filled my entire being as I painfully realized I had no idea what to do next.

What about my career? I thought. What about the solo hiking trips I had painstakingly researched, the itineraries saved in my travel folder the previous night?

My thoughts spiraled out of control. What about my life? What about my family? "Do I have to tell anyone about this, or can we just keep this a stupid little secret, dumb tumor?" I begged with it. I pleaded with it. I told that tumor, "You are not welcome here. I'm too busy for you and the suffering you've already started to bring."

The problem with this tumor, however, was that like its unobliging host, it was persistent and goal oriented. The tumor had no intention of coming to a reasonable agreement with me. It wanted to stay in my brain and torment me, scare me, make me suffer.

I think I heard the tumor say to me at one point, "Your life will never be the same, lady. This is what you get for thinking you had everything under control. Don't you realize you are in control of nothing?" The tumor laughed at me.

The first time I realized just how true this was, I felt fear. Now, this realization makes me feel absolutely, utterly free.

Over the following months, I learned that thinking we are in control can only bring us momentary happiness when we seem to be winning the game—when, for the briefest of impermanent moments, we are outsmarting cancer cells, viruses, suffering that will inevitably enter all our lives when we least expect it. If we are prepared for the impermanence of everything, the constant change that our lives will bring, we can find a peaceful freedom in letting go and letting life happen.

Outside the imaging center, standing on a busy street in downtown Chiang Mai next to a McDonald's filled with American tourists, I started to pace back and forth. I realized I should be admitted to the hospital. Today, right now. I should not be standing alone on the sidewalk in Chiang Mai, waiting for a grand mal seizure to come along and kill me. I texted a picture of my scan to Dr. Pertha and told her it looked like a tumor or an abscess. I requested to be admitted to the hospital that day. Dr. Pertha agreed and arranged for me to have a direct admission to the hospital later that afternoon.

In the meantime, still standing in shock outside the imaging center, I called Sean. "Hey, how are you? Did you find anything out?" he asked nervously.

"Sean, it's not good. It's actually very, very bad," I told him. "It looks like I have a giant brain tumor."

"What the hell? Courtney, are you OK? I'm three blocks away from you at a Starbucks. Come here, show me the pictures, and we'll make a plan," he told me.

I found Sean sitting in a window seat of a sunny, beautiful Starbucks café. He had the day off because a mysterious virus that had originated in Wuhan had just found its way to Thailand. Sean's clinic director didn't want to expose him to this unknown risk.

As he scrolled through the images on my phone, I watched his eyes grow wider, filled with knowledge he didn't want to have. He didn't have to say anything. His eyes told me he agreed with my diagnosis. A silent tear rolled down my cheek.

In a state of prescient brilliance, Sean suggested we should walk to my apartment and pack up all my things. At that point, I hadn't even considered that I would spend more than one night in the hospital.

Unfortunately, Sean was right; I would never again return to my gorgeous, sun-filled Chiang Mai apartment. I would never again be the same person, either. This was my first lesson in nonself (*anatta* in Pali, an ancient and sacred language of Buddhism), a Buddhist concept that there is no separate, permanently existing, intrinsic entity. Buddhists believe that our fictional idea of an autonomous, separate *me* that we control is ultimately the root of our suffering. Rather than "I, me, mine," Buddhists practice selflessness and find comfort in the impermanence of all things, including the false perception of a permanent *me*.

The two of us packed up the entire apartment in ten minutes, stuffing all my clothes, my shoes, my precious souvenirs, and my previous identity into two large suitcases. Sean became my hero and lifelong friend over the upcoming forty-eight hours, and I have never been able to thank him enough for all that he did for me while I alternated between emotions of denial and shock.

I don't remember taking a cab to the hospital, but Sean must have called one and loaded my bags into it because soon, we were standing at the hospital entrance. Instead of heading in to work, we were given hand sanitizer and masks to protect us from the new virus before we were allowed to proceed into the hospital.

Dr. Pertha met us in the hospital lobby and guided us upstairs to the same neurology clinic I had been in that very morning. The clinic was now dimly lit, empty, and eerily quiet apart from the frantic typing of Dr. Nera, still hard at work. The two doctors spoke quickly to each other in Thai.

I have only wonderful things to say about the medical care I received in Thailand. My own medical opinions were graciously accepted into the care plan. I sensed one major difference, however, between medical customs in Thailand and in America. In Thailand, many patients tend to agree with their physician's recommendations with few questions asked. As a physician in America, I often encounter a very different patient response. At home, patients are encouraged to be their own best advocates, to ask questions and offer suggestions about what they want their medical plan to look like. As a physician myself, I was in an extraordinarily unique position where I could medically and personally advocate for myself. Unfortunately, I could do so only in English.

Our strange physician group discussed a hospital admission plan together. We all agreed that a brain tumor was the most likely diagnosis, but an infection was still a possibility. We decided I would be started immediately on an antiepileptic medication to prevent seizures, high-dose steroids to reduce brain swelling, and an antibiotic.

After the plan was made, Dr. Nera told me to wait in the lobby for a few minutes until the transport team could take me in a wheelchair to my room. I could walk, but this was protocol.

With a few minutes to myself, I suddenly realized I would have to tell my family what had happened. The last time I'd spoken with them was the previous day. I had called my mom and told her, "I don't want to worry you, but I'm having some unusual symptoms and am going to the doctor tomorrow just to make sure everything is OK." Of course, I'm sure she was terribly worried, but I had tried to dodge specifics and keep conversation light. What good would it do, I thought, to tell my mother I was worried I was having seizures in a foreign country?

Yet now here I was, standing in a hospital in Chiang Mai, waiting for a medical team to wheel me up to a hospital room where I would spend the night being monitored for additional seizures triggered by the large tumor in my skull. I had to tell my parents. The situation seemed impossible.

Abandoning caution and cost, I turned my cell service on, figuring this was an emergency situation. It was now early evening in Thailand. With the time difference, I calculated it was around 7:00 a.m. in Minnesota. I decided to call my parents before they left for work that day. Phone ringing, I sat alone in the corner of the waiting room, occasionally sending nervous glances to Sean as he smiled back at me reassuringly.

"Hi, honey, how are you?" my mom answered.

My voice shook as I tried to get out my words as concisely and clearly as possible before the point where I knew I would break down and start to sob. "Mom, is Dad home too? I need to tell you both something."

My dad hopped on the line as I heard my mom switch our call to speakerphone. "Hey, Court! What's going on? Everything OK?" he asked, somewhat frantically.

"I have some bad news. Are you sitting down?" I asked them. "You know how I mentioned I was having some odd symptoms the other day?"

"Yes, you said some strange muscle cramping and a fever. Why? Did it get worse?" my mom asked anxiously.

"Well, today, I went to the doctor here in Thailand. I ended up needing an MRI for my symptoms, which turned out to be seizures. I don't know how to tell you this," I said, "but the scan showed a brain tumor. I'll be a patient in the hospital here tonight and will update you as soon as I know more."

Silence and quiet sobbing followed. "Keep us updated; we're here for you. We will tell your brother, don't worry," my dad reassured me.

I hung up from the strangest call of my life just in time for a team of nurses and transport staff to arrive to take me to my hospital room. Sean walked with us as I sat in the wheelchair, in shock.

As a female patient and physician, I was fortunate to receive a private room on the eleventh floor during my hospital stay, a true luxury at that hospital. I was shocked to see in front of me a large hospital room, equivalent in size to an urban studio apartment, complete with bed, sitting area, and kitchenette. There was a huge, open-air balcony with surprisingly low railings, over which I could see the glorious, recently summitted Doi Suthep Mountain in the distance. Golden light reflected off the chedi of Wat Phra That into my hospital room, blanketing me in comfort.

Thinking we should be able to have a life without any suffering
is as deluded as thinking we should be able to have a left
side without a right side . . . "Right, you have to go away. I
don't want you. I only want the left"—that's nonsense . . .
If there's no right, then there's no left. Where there is no
suffering, there can be no happiness either, and vice versa.

—Thich Nhat Hanh

୫

I often think back on that day and wonder, could I go back to that morning and enjoy one last mug of coffee without knowing what was to come? Would stalling my diagnosis have changed anything? Does postponing inevitable suffering make us suffer less?

I've decided that the answer is no. Postponing suffering will not end suffering. Suffering will find us when it wants to. If we forget it's coming, we may think we have outsmarted it, only to have it find and destroy us when we least expect it.

I learned over the upcoming months that instead of postponing inevitable suffering, we should "embrace the suck," a military slang term meaning to consciously accept or appreciate something that is extremely unpleasant but unavoidable for forward progress. In more eloquent terms, I believe this means we should try to find small moments of joy and happiness even in the midst of suffering, which can make our suffering more manageable. A family friend once told me her motto was "Never postpone joy." I liked this. But I offer the reverse. Never postpone suffering, because without suffering, we cannot truly experience joy.

When we finally realize, perhaps at age eighty, perhaps at twenty-nine, or perhaps now, that a tiny virus or a sneaky cancer cell has been secretly plotting to take control over the comfortable life we've worked so hard to create, will we still be able to be happy?

When suffering finds us someday, like it found me in that MRI machine in Thailand, will we let it take over, or will we have a strategy to find joy in spite of it? How do we find happiness in a world where suffering continues to exist and always will?

As the soft golden glow of Wat Phra That Doi Suthep shone into my hospital room, I lay in bed. A nurse placed an IV in my arm and brought me three new pills to swallow. I was a patient. I was a physician. I was lost—or was I found?

10

A patient in Thailand

*Time never waits but keeps flowing. Not only does
time flow unhindered, but correspondingly our
lives too keep moving onward all the time.*

—the Dalai Lama

The evening of my hospital admission, I saw one nurse. She gave me
my new medications and told me to push a call button if I needed
her. This was not my first time as a patient, although it had been
many years since I last was one, and I had definitely never been
one in a foreign country. I had also never experienced the strange
juxtaposition of being a patient and a physician simultaneously.

As an internal medicine–trained physician, I am extremely
comfortable in the hospital setting. I went through residency planning to spend my career working as a hospitalist, an internal medicine physician who spends all his or her time practicing medicine
solely in the hospital setting, helping to admit, treat, and discharge
adult patients with a variety of illnesses.

Although the medical care system works differently in Thailand
than in America, many of the basic logistical and scheduling aspects
of my hospital stay were familiar to me. I knew that the physician
would order initial labs and vital sign checks, so I was prepared when
the lab technician came into my room, stuck an IV in me, and took
a few vials of blood without saying a word. I was also mentally prepared to be woken up from sleep every few hours for vital signs, routine monitoring of my heart rate, blood pressure, and oxygen levels.

Every time a familiar activity happened, I felt grateful. *OK, I know what this is. I can feel the blood pressure cuff squeezing my arm. I can read my blood pressure measurement, I know this number is OK.* When an IV pole was wheeled into my room and fluids were hung next to me, I thought, *OK, this is a familiar intravenous fluid. I know why the physician ordered this and I know what effects it will have on me.* None of this was explained to me as it was happening, partly because of the language barrier, but more honestly because none of this is ever really explained well to patients.

As a physician, I often make the decision to order labs, place IV lines, start fluids, and do vital sign checks without informing my patients of these decisions. Of course, I always inform my patients of critical changes in their treatment plans or test results; however, routine tasks such as those above are as commonplace in medicine as sending an email would be in the corporate world. Physicians do not always remember that for patients, an email feels very different than a blood draw or a blood pressure measurement.

As a physician, I knew I would likely not receive any lab or imaging results for at least twenty-four hours. I also knew I would only have a few minutes to ask my hospital physician all my daily questions before he would need to move on to see another, sicker patient.

Waking up in the hospital the following morning was a sharp contrast from the luxurious king bed in the chic apartment I had recently come to call home. A knock on the door told me breakfast had arrived. The nurse had kindly selected the American breakfast menu option, which consisted of a cold hot dog and cold French fries.

I made a list of questions to ask Dr. Nera before he arrived. I was grateful I knew to do this and wasn't taken by surprise when he was in and out of my room in less than five minutes. Throughout all these familiar steps, I continuously found myself feeling one overarching emotion: gratefulness.

I absolutely cannot fathom how terrifying it would be to be a patient, let alone a patient in a foreign country, lying alone in a hospital room undergoing the above procedures without knowing why these things happen, when they happen, or what the results mean. The only reason I felt comfortable in this situation was that it is literally my day-to-day job. I can't imagine the fear a patient would feel experiencing these things with no grasp on the language and no underlying framework of the way hospitals work.

I tell you all this not because it is how medicine should be, how it always is, or how it always will be, but because I cannot deny how profoundly grateful I felt to understand the situation around me through the eyes of a physician.

Being a patient is terrifying. As a patient, autonomy is gone. You find yourself with a million unanswered questions, and you spend hours waiting for a physician you just met to tell you the worst news of your life.

I hope that I always remember this hospital admission with absolute clarity and precision so that I may act as a more compassionate physician to my own patients. In the end, one of the greatest difficult gifts of my global medicine experience was actually my experience being a patient. Through this, I learned to be a better physician. I realized that knowledge is power. I decided then that when I was back at work, I would try to spend a few extra minutes with my own patients and provide them with knowledge to feel safe, respected, and understood, rather than afraid and confused.

On the second day of my hospitalization, I was mesmerized by a small gecko who decided to live in the hospital bathroom. He was black and kind of cute. He liked to sleep under the sink and didn't move much, but his presence was strangely appreciated. To this day, Sean assures me this was not a steroid-induced hallucination. Sean stayed with me in my hospital room the entire time I was there. He remembers the gecko. He remembers my tears.

Around noon, I started crying and simply couldn't stop. Sean lay next to me, comforting me. He did not say anything because there was simply nothing to say. As my sobs quieted, he stepped away; an hour later, he returned with a hot chestnut latte, a bowl of spicy pad thai, and various chocolate bars for my choosing.

As I lay in bed eating chocolate, crying, and updating my family and friends back home, Sean was my constant advocate. He gathered up all my paper medical records from the nursing station and my MRI imaging results, all written in Thai, and brought them back to my room. "What are you doing?" I asked him in a state of shock and confusion.

"We need to figure out how to get you home. We need to find a neurosurgeon who can help you," Sean said confidently. I listened as he proceeded to call every neurologist and neurosurgeon he had ever worked with in America to discuss this interesting case with them.

"You don't have to do all this for me," I told Sean, who simply smiled and continued to work.

Sean's persistence led us to a brilliant neurosurgeon, Dr. Clair,* whom I had never met but who happened to work for my home institution, the University of Minnesota. Dr. Clair called me in the middle of the night in America to talk me through his plan. He told me I should be rushed home to Minnesota, be kept stabilized on antiepileptics and steroids, and undergo an urgent brain surgery upon my return. He said I needed a brain biopsy to decipher precisely what kind of tumor this was. With that call, Dr. Clair ruled out the very small possibility of a brain abscess, and I started to process my new reality.

Sean made endless calls to our clinic directors back home. Together, my advocates in Thailand and Minnesota arranged for a medical evacuation flight, set to depart in forty-eight hours. Somehow, Sean worked tirelessly to send my entire medical file to a representative at my international medical insurance company, who quickly emailed me an airline ticket for a first-class seat on Delta One for the most unexpected ending to my journey.

I realized two things that day. First, an acquaintance can quickly become a friend; and second, sometimes, life is far more exciting than any fictional story you can write. My novel inspiration came at me, strong and unrelenting. So I wrote.

11

A monk and an amulet

Sometimes, we look at the negative side of things and then feel hopeless. This, I think, is a wrong view.

—the Dalai Lama

I woke up in my hospital bed the following day, suddenly realizing this was my last day in Thailand. My journey had come to an abrupt and unexpected end—although, when I think about it now, my real journey was only just beginning.

My work with the palliative medicine clinic had introduced me to an incredible team of nurses, physicians, and social workers, all experts in tough conversations about chronic disease, death, and dying. Ms. A was one of these superwomen. Ms. A and a group of my palliative care friends visited me in the hospital. These women laughed with me, cried with me, ate food with me, and most importantly, listened to me. I owe them more thanks than I can ever say.

Prior to my hospitalization, one of the things I was most looking forward to in Thailand was the opportunity to have a "monk chat." Many temples in Thailand advertise times when monks are available to have free, informal chats with interested visitors. These chats offer a dedicated and casual experience where people can ask a monk anything they feel could be helpful. I'd had "monk chat" noted on my calendar every day since my arrival in Thailand; unfortunately, I kept postponing this chat for other adventures.

In preparation for my eventual monk chat, I kept an evolving list of my questions on my phone. They included:

- "What is one thing worth giving up to relieve yourself from suffering?"

- "What is the key to finding peace within yourself?"

- "How do you make peace with your decisions, especially those that have hurt others?"

- "How does one find happiness in a world of endless suffering?"

Lying in the hospital bed that day in Thailand, I realized I'd never made it to my monk chat. As I looked at these questions, I started to cry. At that moment, more than ever before, I needed guidance. I needed answers. I needed a way to find peace and happiness in order to cope with my unexpected suffering.

When the palliative care heroes stopped by again later than afternoon, they asked if there was anything else they could do for me. One common role of a palliative care team is to provide spiritual guidance for a patient when requested. In America, palliative teams often help coordinate with chaplains or call in priests to administer "last rites." In Thailand, there are not many priests; however, there are many monks. I asked my palliative care friends for one favor that day. "Can you find a monk to stop by and talk with me before I leave?" I asked.

An hour after these superwomen left my room, a middle-aged monk in a saffron robe walked into my hospital room with Ms. A following closely behind. The monk clasped his hands together in prayer and bowed to me so low I feared he would topple over. He spoke some English, but Ms. A was there to interpret when needed.

I sat across from the monk and told him about my brain tumor. He listened to my story with hands resting calmly on his lap, smiling the whole time. After I'd finished, the monk spoke in English, summarizing everything I ever needed to know about life in two minutes.

In these two minutes, the monk, whose name I now cannot remember, said to me, "Be happy." I nodded, unsure of what to say. "Find time to calm the mind," he went on.

I let this sink in. Be happy? Had this monk forgotten I'd just told him I had a brain tumor? He went on to say, "This happened for a reason. Smile. Do not cry."

Hearing this, of course, I burst into tears and smiled foolishly at the same time. Every emotion was coursing through my veins: fear, happiness, sadness, terror, joy.

The wise monk saw my tears and said, "Do not worry about your illness. Illness and death are a natural part of life."

I had never in my life felt the kind of deep inner peace I felt when the monk spoke those two brief sentences. Illness and death are a natural part of life. As a physician, I knew this, of course, yet I had never actually considered that this fact of life would also apply to me. I'm young and healthy, why would I be dying? *How foolish,* I thought—*we are all dying.* Death had found me, and I was not prepared for it.

The monk was right. How simple, yet profound. I have had what feels like hundreds of years of schooling, yet nothing in my education was as helpful to me as this monk's brief lesson. As a physician who has seen illness and death more times than I can count, I can tell you without a doubt that only one thing is medically certain in this life, and that is death.

Why fear the inevitable? Why keep quiet about death when every human being in the world will experience it? Humans, especially in the West, do not seem to like talking about death. It's as if we think that if we ignore death, we can potentially avoid it. Yet we know deep down this is a fallacy. Death will find us eventually. If we are prepared for it, won't it be so much easier to accept?

12

Life is a vacation

The maximum duration of a human life is [around] one hundred years, which, compared to the life of the planet, is very short. This brief existence should be used in such a way that it does not create pain for others. It should be committed not to destructive work but to more constructive activities . . . in this way, our brief span as a tourist on this planet will be meaningful. If a tourist visits a certain place for a short period and creates more trouble, this is silly. But if as a tourist you make others happy during this short period, that is wise.

—the Dalai Lama

Not one of us will get out of this life alive, no matter what brilliance science and medicine can come up with. Yet in the West, people rarely want to discuss death. My patients come to me to fix them, to help them, rarely acknowledging that the ending of their illness may be death. It's rare that I hear a patient, family member, or friend say, "When I'm gone . . ." or, "After I die, please . . ."

For something that every single human being has in common, it is curious to me that we almost unanimously dislike talking about death, at least in the Western world. Perhaps this has to do with our culture, our religions, our focus on the "American dream," which seems more inspirational when focused on success while living than when focused on success through acceptance of the fact that we are dying.

At age twenty-nine, I was given an abrupt reminder that my

time on this earth is limited. At first, this scared me, shocked me, saddened me.

Over time, my perspective shifted. Wouldn't life, and therefore death, be so much calmer, so much simpler, if we could just admit that life and death always go together? When we deny that death is coming to us and to others, it seems we only increase our eventual suffering.

When I returned home to Minnesota, I bought a book called *Advice on Dying and Living a Better Life* by His Holiness the Dalai Lama. A friend saw this book on my bookshelf and rolled her eyes at me. "Why would you buy such a depressing book?" she asked. I just smiled. To me, nothing about this book looked depressing. It looked fascinating. The summary on the back of the book says, "The Dalai Lama offers new inspiration on a subject that we, in the West, have long ignored to our detriment. It is only by taming our minds and fully facing the end of our lives that we can fully live in the present moment."

How beautiful, how simple. I vowed after my diagnosis to stop ignoring the inevitable and start loving every tiny bit of my boring, stressful, wonderful, incredible life.

In *Advice on Dying and Living a Better Life*, the Dalai Lama compares our lives to a brief time as tourists on this planet. This idea speaks to me. Imagine your last trip. Wherever you went, did you go to create trouble? Probably not. Did you go to make you or others happy? I imagine so.

Why, then, shouldn't we think of our life on earth as one exciting, hopefully fulfilling trip? Whatever your religious or non-religious beliefs, we can all likely agree our time here is limited. We are visitors. We are tourists taking a hundred-year trip (in my case, perhaps a forty-year trip) on this fantastic planet. We should respect the earth. We are here to make ourselves and others happy, not to create trouble.

These words made me think we should live our lives like we're on the greatest vacation of all time. There's no reason to be sad on vacation. Use your life, your brief span as a tourist on this planet, to find happiness.

At the time, I did not yet have this perspective. Sitting there in the hospital room on my last day in Thailand, the monk noticed me starting to cry harder. He asked, "What are you still worried about?"

Between sobs, I said, "I'm worried about my family. I think I can deal with this, but I can't stand thinking about how sad my family will be when I die." The tears streamed down my face then and stream down my face now as I type this.

The wise monk said calmly, "I understand." He paused, then went on, "Try to find happiness and spread this happiness to everyone around you. Your family will be OK. If you can find happiness and share it with them, you can take away their sadness." These words became my mission. These words radically changed my perspective on life.

At that moment, Ms. A reached into her bag and pulled out an amulet, a small, round piece of plaster with the form of Buddha molded on it, covered by a plastic case. In the Thai Buddhist tradition, an amulet is considered a sacred item. It is often purchased to help raise money for a particular temple. Ms. A told me that amulets are worn as necklaces by many Buddhist practitioners as ornaments of good fortune, protection, and health.

I took the amulet in my hand. Ms. A told me the monk would say a prayer to bless it and me. Clasping our hands together, we all bowed together as the monk began to melodically recite a beautiful sutra, or Buddhist scripture. Although I understood none of the words, I understood every bit of the meaning. Still crying, still smiling, I watched as the monk smiled back at me and repeated his words, "Be happy. Smile, do not cry."

He left the room, and I hugged Ms. A goodbye. "Keep in touch. You will be just fine," she told me.

Placing the amulet on a chain, I slipped it around my neck, where it hangs to this day, reminding me of the profound happiness we can find in this life, even in the darkest of times.

13

———

Home

You must not consider tolerance and patience to be
signs of weakness. I consider them signs of strength.

—the Dalai Lama

My flight was scheduled to leave Thailand late in the evening. I would arrive home to Minneapolis nearly forty-eight hours later. Given the heightened seizure risk that came with altitude change, my international health insurance team arranged for a physician named Adi* to accompany me on my journey home.

This was my first experience with a medical flight companion, and I assure you I will never forget it. Adi was a middle-aged physician from India. He walked into my hospital room late that evening and introduced himself to me with a friendly smile. I quickly learned that Adi loved to talk. He began to tell me about his life story in intricate detail without any probing whatsoever. I had never before learned so much about another person in such a short period of time without asking any questions.

Adi told me he had trained in critical care and emergency medicine but quit his regular job to start a medical transportation business. Instead of working at a hospital, he spends his time flying coach from his home in India to various parts of the world to accompany a patient to their destination in first class. This career honestly sounded fascinating to me.

Without asking, Adi told me that he rarely has to use his medical skills. Usually, patients do fine on flights. One time, however,

Adi said his patient had significant trouble breathing and had to be emergently intubated on the plane. Another time, his patient had a heart attack and required an emergency landing, which the pilots were not thrilled about.

From the very start, I had concerns about Adi's ability to get us safely home. When we arrived at the Chiang Mai airport, he could not find his passport, and we spent quite some time rummaging through his bags to dig it out. When we boarded our first flight, headed to Seoul, Adi was seated right next to me. He talked for the entire three-hour flight. I learned that he had two children, both living in the United States. He was very excited that my destination was in the United States; this meant he could spend an extra day visiting his children after he got me safely to Minnesota. I learned that Adi loved to shop. He loved to buy expensive watches. He had a fascination for women from parts of the world unlike his home.

When we landed in Seoul, Adi told me we had access to the priority lounge with our first-class tickets. We spent the four-hour layover relaxing in the lounge, with Adi enjoying multiple plates of food from the complimentary snack and dessert buffets. He asked, "Why aren't you eating? Aren't you hungry?" at least a dozen times before I finally grabbed a plate and ate a few bites to appease him. In actuality, I was not hungry because we had been fed an extravagant meal on our first flight and I was also somewhat anxious about my brain tumor.

Around thirty minutes before we were set to board our next flight, I realized I was hearing an unfamiliar sound: silence. I looked over at Adi, asleep in the chair next to me. As time went on, I started to get nervous that we would miss our flight. I coughed loudly until Adi opened his eyes and asked me, "What time is it? Do you know when our next flight boards?"

I stared at him, unable to fully comprehend what he was asking me, his patient. When Adi couldn't find his boarding pass in his

bag to check the departure time, I handed him my neatly orga-
nized boarding pass and passport folio and showed him that we
were scheduled to board in fifteen minutes.

Adi quickly grabbed his bags, jumped up, and asked me to
come with him to a duty-free store before we boarded the next
flight. His girlfriend, he said, would be expecting a gift when he
got to the United States—though he had already told me on our
previous flight that he was married to a lovely woman back home.
I kept quiet and spent the next ten minutes helping Adi pick out
a perfume from the duty-free store, thinking, *Maybe I'm not so upset
about my own divorce after all.*

Our thirteen-hour flight from Seoul to Detroit could have been
excruciatingly painful if Adi and I were seated next to one another. Fortunately, Delta One seats on long international flights
are situated in individual pods with privacy doors. I closed my
door and shut my eyes. Although I was forbidden from enjoying
the free booze on the flight, I thoroughly enjoyed a cheese platter,
a salmon dinner, and a dessert tray. I spent a few hours watching
movies and unknowingly selected one about a woman dying of a
brain tumor. I proceeded to bawl my eyes out behind the privacy
door.

Around ten hours into the flight, the attendant announced
a medical emergency on the speaker overhead: "Any physicians
on board, please go to row thirty-four to assist if able." I looked
back at Adi, who let the flight attendant know he was a physician
and volunteered to help. Thirty minutes later, a second medical
emergency was announced overhead. These were the early days
of COVID-19, and many people were developing their first symptoms on our flight.

Knowing Adi was already helping another patient, I volunteered to help the second time. I was starting to get confused about
my role. *I am a patient,* I thought, *but I'm also a physician.* Physician
came first. I found the patient who needed help, and Adi met me

there. He forbade me from helping, saying, "You are my patient and you can't risk catching this virus." This was smart advice, knowing what we know now about COVID-19, but it discouraged me nonetheless.

Reluctantly, I walked back to my seat. Adi came over a few minutes later and ran through the patient cases with me, appreciating my insight and advice as a colleague. After this discussion, he offered me a job as a traveling physician with his company. I thanked him and said, "I'll let you know how things are going after brain surgery."

After landing in Detroit, we spent another three-hour layover eating and talking in a priority lounge. Here, Adi lost his boarding passes once again, and his phone ran out of battery. After I lent him my phone charger and found his boarding passes near the food buffet, we were ready to board the final flight, from Detroit to Minneapolis.

At one point, I became slightly worried that Adi was developing a little unrequited crush on me, and I decided it was time for a nap. Two hours later, wheels touched down in Minneapolis. I found myself standing in a familiar airport, hearing a familiar language, and picking up familiar bags from the carousel with an unfamiliar traveling companion next to me and an unfamiliar tumor in my head.

Adi told me we were supposed to find a driver who would bring us straight to the hospital. After looking through many text messages, however, he appeared confused. "Arrivals Door 4" flashed on his phone screen. I told Adi I could get us there, and he followed me through the busy airport until we found our driver. I promise you I'm not making this up, but somehow, our driver's GPS wouldn't work on his phone. Fortunately, I happened to know the way to the hospital from the airport.

I directed our driver to the University of Minnesota. Thanking me, he parked outside the main lobby and unloaded our bags. I knew I would be a patient in the neurosurgical ICU, as Dr. Clair had already told me this on the phone. Fortunately, I had worked in that area of the hospital many times before.

"Adi," I said, "I know where to go, follow me." We walked to the front desk of the neurosurgical ICU, and I told the charge nurse the brief version of my story.

"Ah, yes," she said. "We knew you would be arriving from Thailand but didn't know what time." She ushered me to my hospital room, where I said goodbye to Adi. He hugged me and handed me his business card. "Call me when all this is over and you're feeling good. It would be great to work with you," he said.

I love these memories of my flight home with Adi. It was all so surreal; I often think I must have dreamt it.

I closed the door of my hospital room, a room I was quite familiar with as a physician, and sat down on the bed as a neurosurgical patient for the very first time.

14

Physician becomes patient

Resilient trees can weather a violent storm
because their roots are deep and firm.

—Thich Nhat Hanh

Shortly after my hospital admission, I heard a knock on the door. Three of my best girlfriends, Marisa, Kari, and Stephanie, walked in carrying flowers, cards, and baskets of gifts. We all started crying together instantly.

I met Marisa on my first day of high school. On day one, our lockers were next to each other. As we opened them up simultaneously, we realized we had the same English class on our morning schedule. After English class, we returned to our lockers. Immediately, Marisa whispered, "I think I have a huge crush on the boy who was sitting next to you in class." I giggled and told her, "No way. I think I'm in love with the boy who was sitting next to you in class." Our ninth-grade loves went unrequited, but Marisa and I started a friendship of love that has only grown stronger over the past fifteen years.

At my first wedding, Marisa was my maid of honor. In her speech, she talked about how happy she was that the bride had found the love of her life at such an early age. James and I smiled at each other, blushing, until Marisa cracked a stellar joke. "Of course, I am referring to the love between Courtney and me, which started from the first day of high school and has only continued to get stronger."

The audience cracked up. Five years later, now divorced from James but still best friends with Marisa, I realize just how right she really was.

I also met Kari, another of my best friends, in the ninth grade. Kari and I were in the high school choir together. I vividly remember looking across the room during our first choir rehearsal and locking eyes with a badass, beautiful, confident young woman who I knew from the start absolutely hated me. I looked away, terrified to have accidentally disturbed her personal space with my eyes.

As surprising as this is to say about teenage girl behavior, I soon realized that Kari did not hate me, and we became fast friends. Kari was tall, athletic, and effortlessly cool. She still is. This woman is a fantastic veterinarian, mother, performer (she still sings even though I lost my nerve to perform ages ago), and friend. In fact, this book is dedicated to Nora, Kari's first child and my spiritual daughter, or Buddhist goddaughter, who is already every bit as sassy, loving, and bold as her fantastic mama is.

Finally, let me introduce you to Stephanie. Stephanie entered my life later in the game than the other two, but she is every bit as important to me. She is an internal medicine physician whom I met in my second year of residency. We were sitting in the resident lounge at the hospital one day and had both finished work early. For no clear reason, I turned to Steph and asked, "Do you like wine? Let's go get a glass of wine somewhere."

Steph looked up at me. "I love wine. I have a wine-tasting notebook in my bag. Let's do it." We discussed our shared love of wine over a glass of rich Bordeaux, giggling hysterically as we joked that the tasting notes consisted predominately of *grapes*, and decided to continue our friend date into the dinner hour. "Where have you been hiding all my life?" we both wondered. It's no easy task to find new friends as an adult. Steph and I were lucky enough to do this, and I thank the universe for the bit of good karma that brought her into my life.

In addition to these three stellar women, there are so many other important friends in my life. I would not be the person I am today without my friends and their literally never-ending love and support. I mention these three women because, in part due to location, they were able to be with me physically during my first surgical experience and recovery. I know many others were there with me in spirit, and I am forever grateful.

As soon as Kari, Stephanie, and Marisa streamed into my room, they piled onto my hospital bed and hugged me. Tears rolling down our faces, Steph opened up a gift she had brought, which included new cozy pajamas and slippers. As I changed into my comfy outfit, Marisa set up the small hospital bedside table with endless treats: chocolates, cookies, chips, sparkling water, fruit. Kari arranged beautiful flowers in a makeshift vase, really a plastic suction container hanging from the hospital wall. As we sat together, intermittently crying and giggling, my fears evaporated.

The majority of my four-night hospital stay was uneventful. After one stable night in the intensive care unit, I was moved upstairs to the general neurological floor. As a patient in the hospital where I also work as a physician, I was worried at first about an awkward, confusing experience.

As resident physicians, nurses, hospital staff, residency administrators, family members, and friends streamed into my hospital room, however, I quickly realized how grateful I was to be surrounded by familiar faces. My room became a new, unexpected lounge where colleagues spent time socializing, eating treats they brought me, and laughing about strange patient encounters.

I was sitting in the hospital bed, but I was still part of the physician team. My colleagues did not abandon me; they embraced and supported me.

Throughout every interaction in the hospital, I remembered the words the wise monk had told me. "Smile. Do not cry. Spread happiness to the people around you." I found that the more I leaned into this—the more I smiled and laughed with my visitors—the more they smiled and laughed with me. I found that smiling, laughter, and joy are much better shared experiences than sadness and fear could ever be. Emotions are contagious, so I chose to spread happy ones.

None of this is to say that I ignored or suppressed my feelings. Of course, I felt some sadness, confusion, and fear. But greater than all these emotions, I felt joy. I felt love, kindness, and compassion from more people than I could count. Just as I did not feel I deserved a bag of cookies from my first patient in Thailand, I felt then that I did not deserve such an incredible outpouring of love at home.

15

Wait, I might die?

A place to stay untouched by death
Does not exist.
It does not exist in space, it does not exist in the ocean,
Nor in the middle of a mountain.

—the Buddha

I woke up in the hospital thinking about the undeniable interconnectedness of life and death. As family, friends, and colleagues stopped by my hospital room, I became more and more fascinated by their various reactions as I started to discuss the high probability that my brain tumor could be cancer. Even more curious were their reactions when I casually brought up the subject of death. Perhaps it was the jet lag or the abrupt cultural transition back home, but I had forgotten how uncomfortable many people are talking about death in America.

Dr. Clair and his neurosurgical team came to meet me within hours of my return to Minnesota, and I quickly decided that my brain would be literally in good hands. I was scheduled for the operating room in three days—the surgeons told me they needed to give the swelling in my brain time to settle down before they drilled a hole in my skull.

As a physician, I knew the risks of this procedure—I could simply wake up with a mild headache or have a much more severe complication. This surgery brought a risk of stroke, loss of motor function, loss of speech, and death. This was my brain, after all.

There was a chance I would leave surgery permanently unconscious, requiring machines to keep me alive. This was something I absolutely, under no circumstances, wanted to happen.

This was the time to talk openly about death. I knew this. I wanted my friends and family to know that death was a possibility for me, not hypothetically, but literally. I did not want to bring them suffering, but I did want to prepare them for a possible reality I had already accepted.

I noticed that my physician friends reacted calmly to these discussions of death, whereas my nonmedical visitors often shifted uncomfortably in their seats, avoiding eye contact, possibly regretting their decision to visit me. They were probably realizing that while they were prepared to say, "Get better soon," with cards and balloons, they were not prepared for what I really needed them to say: "We understand you might die."

Physicians deal with death on a routine basis. We are trained to discuss death, see death, and think about death. I would say as a total generalization that the majority of well-trained internal medicine physicians are comfortable talking about death and dying. I would also assume that most physicians understand the inevitability of death, even their own, and are not as afraid to acknowledge this fact as nonmedical people often are. The truth of the matter is this: I have no idea how long I have left to live, and neither does anyone else. What I do know, however, is that our lives will end in death; that is guaranteed.

Three days of lying in bed in the hospital gave me a lot of time to think, to read, and to write. I updated my blog, which by this point had gained quite an unexpected global following. Friends and family kept me company most hours of the day. At one point, my ex-husband even managed to sneak my dog into the hospital to snuggle with me for an evening prior to surgery. As I cuddled my white husky mix named Ridley, she fell asleep in my arms.

"You know Mama is sick, don't you?" I whispered to my calmly sleeping pup, usually anxious and energized. "Thank you for keeping me company." I fell asleep, arms wrapped around my fifty-pound fur baby, and woke two hours later to the sound of my loving family bringing me dinner and packing up the dog to take her home.

After dinner with my family on this last night before surgery, we hugged goodbye. "You will get through this. You are strong and we love you," they reassured me.

After they left, I knew I had one more task, one I had been dreading. It was time for me to fill out my health-care directive, forms that would let my family know my wishes in case of brain death or another bad outcome. I reflected on words of the Buddha, who reportedly said, "A place to stay untouched by death does not exist." Why then, I thought, would I try to prolong my life in a state of misery if death would find me eventually?

What then, I wondered, is the role of a physician? If death is inevitable, a physician's job cannot be to prevent death. Instead, I feel that a physician's primary role is to do the following: extend the quantity of life, improve the quality of life, or both.

Physicians are often faced with the seemingly impossible decision of prioritizing quantity of life over quality of life or vice versa, as it can be nearly impossible to maintain both. A patient with end-stage cancer may be able to have more time if he is willing to start a clinical trial drug. Let's say that this drug promises five more months of life, yet also causes intractable nausea, vomiting, and fatigue. The patient would have to choose quality of days or quantity of days, but it is unlikely he would receive both.

I have worked with patients who say, "Give me the drug; I want more time, and I don't care if that time is miserable as long as I'm alive." Other patients have told me, "I would rather die tomorrow feeling like myself than have months of feeling utterly miserable."

When I have conversations with my patients about death and dying, I try to decipher whether they align more along the quantity or the quality side of things. You may be surprised to hear the variety of answers I have heard. In these difficult discussions, I usually ask the following questions:

"If you are unable to speak for yourself and too ill to make your own health-care decisions, what would you want your family members, friends, and doctors to know?

"Would you want treatments such as cardiac resuscitation, mechanical ventilation, powerful medications, invasive procedures, artificial nutrition, or intravenous fluids to keep your physical body alive for as much time as possible, even if you were unconscious and unresponsive during this time? Or would you want me to focus on your comfort instead? Would you want me to give you medication to take away your pain, even if that may lead to an earlier death? In other words, does the quality of your days matter more, less, or the same as the quantity of your days?"

For some people, these questions spark an obvious answer: "Doctor, of course I want to live as long as possible," or, "Doctor, of course I want to be comfortable." Unfortunately, many times we are required to make these decisions in situations we have not prepared for in advance. Illness does not wait to enter our lives until the time is convenient.

As I sat alone in my dark hospital room with my health-care directive forms on the bed in front of me, tears started to roll down my face. I had filled out these forms many times with my patients, yet I had never really considered the fact that I too would be faced with my own mortality so soon. I knew there was no way I was going under the knife without completing these forms. If I had a stroke, a bleed, or another unexpected outcome leading to permanent unconsciousness, then under no circumstances would I want to be kept alive with machines. I love my brain. I love to think, I love to write, I love to work. If my brain stops working, for me, this would be the equivalent of death.

Filling out a health-care directive as a twenty-nine-year-old previously healthy person was an odd experience to say the least.

Throughout this experience, however, I kept thinking how grateful I was to know about these forms. I was grateful to know that they exist, that they are respected amongst medical providers, and that they gave me the opportunity to make my wishes known while I was still able to articulate them. As a physician, but more importantly as a patient, I find it important to be your own best advocate, both in life and in death.

Tears started to pour down my face as I read through the questions: "If you are permanently unconscious with no likely chance of recovery, would you want your body kept alive with machines?" No, I answered. "Would you like your organs donated?" Yes, I circled. "What would you like your family to know about your wishes for a memorial service after your death?" This one took me a minute. I wrote in the blank space, "Drink some good Italian wine and celebrate for me, with smiles, laughter, and happiness. Try not to be sad. I am at peace with death, and I have had an incredible life thanks to you."

Forms complete and moments after tears stopped flowing down my face, my team of superwomen—Kari, Marisa, and Stephanie—entered my hospital room carrying enough takeout tacos, chips, and guacamole to feed a group of ten. Nonalcoholic sparkling wine in tow, we had a pre–brain surgery celebration. Stephanie had quickly befriended Marisa and Kari, as I'd known she would, and we spent a few hours sharing funny memories, joking about my bad timing in entering the dating pool, and listening to music. We didn't talk much about surgery. As my girlfriends hugged me goodnight, I was again filled with gratitude. "If this is my last night on earth," I told them, "I'm sure as hell thankful to have spent it like this."

As Stephanie left the room, I joked with her, "I probably won't remember you guys after surgery, so make sure you remind me who you are."

She rolled her eyes at me. "Are we that easy to forget?"

16

Just another day of brain surgery

*A crisis has the power to shatter our illusions, to reveal
that in this impermanent world, there really is no
ground to stand on, nothing we can hold on to.*

—Tara Brach, PhD

I woke up the morning of surgery terrified. I took a long, hot shower, thinking perhaps this was the last time I'd be able to stand on my own two feet unassisted for the rest of my life. I let the water fall over me and tried to enjoy the moment.

As I was wheeled down to the preoperative area, I practiced some quiet tonglen meditation. This is my favorite type of meditation, commonly practiced by Buddhists around the world. In tonglen practice, as you breathe in, you imagine yourself breathing in the suffering of another person or an entire community. As you breathe out, you imagine yourself breathing out your compassion, support, and love to help the person suffering. Through my journey, I have found that when I focus on the suffering of others, my own suffering becomes relatively unimportant. With a change in perspective, I realize that I am not the only one on this earth who suffers.

I practiced tonglen aimed at sending compassion to the other patients in the hospital. As I would pass by another patient, I would share a tonglen breath for them. Science is not yet advanced enough to tell us if positive energy, loving thoughts, or compassion can physically impact another individual, yet I can confirm without a doubt that meditating and sending compassion to others helps me calm myself.

My surgery was scheduled for late that evening, and I was alone in my hospital room when the surgeon popped his head in the door around noon and excitedly said, "We were able to move your surgery up! We're ready for you now." I frantically called my parents, brother, and future sister-in-law, who I'm sure ran anxiously to their cars while on the phone as my nurse wheeled me down to the pre-op area. They all arrived to my preoperative room just in time to give me a hug and watch me drift off to sleep.

I do not remember anything from my first surgery. All I remember is waking up in the PACU (post-anesthesia care unit) to see my mother's smiling face above me next to the neurosurgeon, who told me they had successfully taken a biopsy of my right frontal lobe. My mother told me after I was more lucid that she approached to give me a goodnight kiss before she and my father left the hospital. As I was connected from every conceivable angle to monitors and intravenous contraptions, my mother exclaimed, "I want to give you a kiss, but I don't know how to approach you!" She loves to tell me the story of how her "loopy, much-drugged daughter put on her best diva face and gently raised her bare right hand, waving it graciously in front of me."

Apparently, I waved my hand in front of her face for a few moments before declaring, "You may kiss my hand, mother. And by that, I mean my ring."

Suddenly, I saw Stephanie and a few fellow coresidents walk up to the foot of my bed. Giggling at my own hilarious joke before telling it, I looked Stephanie straight in the eyes are said, "Wait, who are you again?" She laughed at my bad joke as I saw a tear roll down her cheek.

My fabulous neurosurgery team came to visit me when I was slightly more alert that evening. They told me I had a "nice-looking brain," which to this day remains my favorite compliment of all time.

Following this, my family left, and I was brought upstairs to recover overnight in the intensive care unit. With monitors beeping continuously and neurologic exams performed every hour, sleep was hard to come by. For most of the night, I joked with my nurses as they sat in my room, asking me questions about the surgery residents they were working with overnight. "Do you think I should page the surgeon with this question a second time, or can it wait?" my nurse asked me.

"Page him again. He should answer that question quickly. And don't feel bad about paging the residents; it is literally our job to respond."

Around 4:00 a.m., after countless neurologic checks and endless beeping of machines, an EKG tech entered my room. "You triggered an alarm because your heart rate is too slow," she told me.

Rolling my eyes, I looked up at my telemetry monitor, which showed sinus bradycardia, a slow heart rate common in young and relatively fit patients. "It's fine," I told her, forgetting I was not the physician in this situation.

"I'm sorry, but I have to take a formal electrocardiogram."

Ten minutes later, with stickers and wires attached to various places on my chest, the EKG machine printed out a very boring EKG. "I'm a doctor, can I see it?" I asked the tech.

Quizzically, she looked over at me and handed me the reading. "It's just sinus bradycardia, nothing to worry about. I'll let my nurse know."

I then proceeded to send what I thought to be a hilarious text to the group of internal medicine residents I work with, joking that a "stat cardiology consult for an asymptomatic, young and healthy patient with sinus bradycardia" would be added to their pile of work in the morning. A few virtual smiles later, I finally fell asleep for a sweet hour of rest.

After my EKG escapade, my neurosurgery team realized that I was doing fairly well postsurgery and decided I could leave the hospital that afternoon. My family came to pick me up, walking slowly with me, an insane-looking girl in pajamas with braids and blood in her hair. The neurosurgeons had braided my hair to keep it out of the way during surgery; I told them if they were ever fired, they could easily have a career as hairstylists.

On the drive home with my parents and brother, I was exhausted. Honestly, I do not remember much apart from an intense craving for a cheeseburger, which my parents appreciated as they stopped to pick one up for me on the way home.

My mother tells a story about what happened as we sat in the car waiting for my father and brother to come out of the restaurant with our burgers. "I knew Courtney was not supposed to be left alone for about forty-eight hours after surgery and should be kept under close observation, so I took this opportunity to casually inquire as to what, precisely, were we looking for as far as postoperative complications go." My mom always laughs as she recalls the next part, where "the doctor answered, not the daughter." Apparently, in my state of delirium and hunger, I told my mom, "Well, that's an excellent question. If I begin speaking unintelligibly, call 911. If I appear to be having a seizure, roll me on my side and call 911. If I become unresponsive, call 911. If fluid begins to come out of my ears or nose, call 911."

My mom paused me at this point. "Fluid?" she asked, eyes wide.

"Yes. It would either be bloody or clear. If it's clear, that could be cerebrospinal fluid," I told her.

"I'm assuming if that happens, I should also call 911?" my mom asked.

"You assume correctly," I replied.

Fortunately, my mom didn't have to call 911 during the next forty-eight hours. I spent this time recovering at my parents' house. My mother, father, brother, and future sister-in-law spoiled me silly. We all had lots of hugs, many laughs, and a surplus of love. We had been given the difficult gift of facing mortality, and we used it to enjoy every moment together.

17

Being human

If you are not aware of death, you will fail to take advantage of this special human life that you have already attained.

—the Dalai Lama

The next morning at 4:00 a.m., I woke up in my childhood bedroom. Immediately alert, it dawned on me that not even a partial craniotomy could cure jet lag. In those early post-op days, I vividly remember waking up every day with the feeling of a terrible hangover, yet I hadn't been able to enjoy any good Chianti in this unfair cycle of events.

High-dose steroids in the immediate days postsurgery led to many wonderful, exciting new symptoms, including severe insomnia, heartburn, weight gain, leg swelling, and extreme hunger. I would routinely wake up in the middle of the night after a vivid dream about breakfast food and absolutely need to make myself a giant stack of pancakes. I'll never forget the most incredibly vivid steroid-induced dream I ever had: I dreamt of a glistening, steaming plate of chicken and waffles. I've never had chicken and waffles in my life. Why this platter of southern comfort food filled my mind and my senses with delight at four in the morning in my childhood bed, I'll never know. But wow, it was a beautiful dream.

After waking up from visions of meat and pastry, I cautiously walked downstairs and found my brother and his fiancée drinking coffee at the kitchen table. "Matt, I had an amazing dream about chicken and waffles," I told him.

"Have you ever even eaten chicken and waffles? That's so random," he said, laughing at me.

"Never in my life. But now I need them."

My brother set down his coffee mug, opened the cupboard, and pulled out a skillet. "I don't think Mom and Dad have the ingredients for early-morning fried chicken, but I'll make you a giant stack of pancakes. Will that do?" My sweet brother. I've never tasted pancakes as good as those.

Over the following days of recovery, I noticed a few things. Recovering from brain surgery is a constant experience of sensory overload. Every sound was louder, every light was brighter, every smell was smellier than before. I spent most of my time lying in bed in a dark room, venturing out only for short walks and frequent snacks, but otherwise enjoying a cave of solitude.

In this cave, I started to think, and I started to write these thoughts down frantically. I reflected on the teachings the wise monk in Thailand had discussed with me. I also started to study. With books of Buddhist philosophy spread around me on my childhood bed and sutures sticking out of the right side of my skull, I tried out a new role: "lunatic postsurgical physician and overzealous student of Buddhist philosophy."

I reflected on the most basic facts of life: I am human. Humans go through remarkably similar life cycles, regardless of ethnicity, race, culture, religion, or geographical location. When you think about it, the life cycle of a human typically consists of four major events: we are born, face challenges, learn something, and die. I am currently somewhere along the spectrum between birth and death. I hate to remind you all, but so are you.

At this point in my recovery, I had many people asking me for specific details about my diagnosis. It took the lab a number of days to decipher the pathology, or laboratory examinations, of the juicy little tumor slices the surgeons had carved from my brain. In the meantime, I reflected on what it felt like to receive a new diagnosis.

Oftentimes, in my role as physician, it is my job to give a patient a new diagnosis. No matter the name—whether it is diabetes, arthritis, depression, or cancer—a new diagnosis is always life changing. A diagnosis is a label which will be plastered on your medical record for the rest of your life, and it can bring fear, questions, concerns, and embarrassment.

Sometimes, if you're lucky, a new diagnosis can bring a sense of peace. It can answer a question about an unusual symptom and offer a label that comforts rather than hurts. More often than not, however, this new label is not experienced with such a positive undertone.

A diagnostic label changes a person. In my case, this label would change my "one-liner," a brief medical description of a patient, from "healthy twenty-nine-year-old female with depression" to "twenty-nine-year-old female with depression and an unspecified brain tumor." Instead of this awful one-liner, I decided to make myself a new one: "twenty-nine-year-old female physician who has always had a quirky brain."

I was happy with this one-liner, this label I had given myself. I accepted it. At that point, I didn't really want to know more. Unfortunately, my surgeon called the next day with pathology results.

"Hi, Courtney. How are you feeling?" Dr. Clair asked slowly.

"I'm fine," I told him. "Recovery is slow but uneventful."

"Unfortunately, I have some bad news," Dr. Clair told me. "We got your biopsy results. You have a glioma, a type of brain cancer. A glioma is a type of brain cancer that starts when glial cells grow too quickly in the brain or spinal cord for unknown reasons. Fortunately, we think yours is low grade."

"Low grade?" I asked, trying and miserably failing to act as both a patient and a knowledgeable physician simultaneously.

"Yes, early stage, where hopefully surgery is all you will need for treatment rather than more aggressive therapies such as chemotherapy or radiation." I soon realized that Dr. Clair was talking about another, more intensive surgery, not the simple biopsy I was still recovering from.

"OK. Thank you for telling me," I said, not sure how else to respond. As a physician, I have given patients bad news hundreds of times. Before this moment, I had never personally received bad news from a physician. *He did a nice job telling me,* I thought. *He was calm, kind.*

Low grade. OK, I can handle low grade. I have cancer, but it might not be so bad. Lots of people have cancer. I started to think of a low-grade glioma as an evil, scheming neighbor who steals my Amazon Prime packages but isn't quite smart enough to figure out my full Social Security number.

Dr. Clair scheduled me a meeting with a neuro-oncologist for the following week to discuss these results in more detail. I sat in my childhood bedroom soaking in my new label: "twenty-nine-year-old physician with depression and brain cancer." Immediately, I thought of my poor family. *How will I tell them?* In this situation, I could not have cared less about my own thoughts on the matter. When given life-altering news, I quickly realized it was a nonnegotiable issue. I had cancer; I could not change that fact. People get cancer. It was nothing I did. It was nothing I didn't do. It was bad luck, that was all. But my family, my poor, loving family . . . this would crush them.

At that moment, I heard the monk whisper in my ear. "*Smile. Do not cry. This happened for a reason.*"

Almost inexplicably, at that moment my primary feeling turned to acceptance. I had never before thought about how I would react when faced with my own mortality, yet here I found myself thinking about the impermanence of life, the impermanence of everything. My primary thoughts were the following: Length of life is not a guarantee. Living, learning, and dying are situations we can count on, but the number of days in between is not something we can predict.

At that moment, I decided that brain cancer or not, I would try to appreciate every single moment of my life. I would smile, not cry. I would share compassion with others, but also with myself. I figured I could spend the next months or years lying in bed curled up in a ball of sadness, or I could embrace life and truly live it. I never want anyone to say, "That girl wasted her time." Instead, I hope they say, "She took her suffering and realized she could use it to find and spread joy." This became my mission.

18

You got this, little snail

The loving mind can observe joy and peace in one moment,
and then grief in the next moment, and it will not be shattered
by the change ... The sky is not affected by the clouds. It is free.

—Sharon Salzberg

Before surgery, I'd requested that my neurosurgeon implant some karate moves into my brain while he was in there. Well, I was starting to lose confidence that the karate moves were in fact coming. I thought I might need to request a refund. Not only was I incapable of cool karate moves, but my body had slowed down to an unfamiliar pace.

A week after surgery, I moved out of my parents' home and back into my own apartment to reestablish a semblance of normalcy. After a month in Thailand and a week in the hospital, it felt incredible to finally be home.

My physicians and parents were nervous for me to be living fully alone so soon after surgery given my heightened risk of seizure or other complication. To appease the group watching cautiously over me, I created a daily calendar with items I found personally hilarious. A sampling of items on this calendar included specific time for writing and snuggling with dog, extreme deadlifting workouts (slow treadmill walks, really), and sleepovers with my night mistresses/protectors/shower guardians. Brain surgery hadn't fully cured my type-A personality.

Marisa, Kari, and Stephanie agreed to take turns spending the night at my apartment, bringing me food, making sure I was stable throughout the night, and sitting on my couch while I showered to make sure I didn't have an unexpected seizure. Looking back, the two weeks of rotating adult slumber parties filled with laughs, snuggles, and joy were some of the most incredible prepandemic presents I could have ever received. In these weeks just before COVID-19 hit the US, I was fortunate enough to spend nearly every waking minute with one of my best friends or family members before social distancing became the new reality.

In the mornings, when my fierce protectors would head to work, I had some time to myself to establish a new recovery routine. Each day, I spent an unbelievably long amount of time walking one block to the local grocery store, packing up as many groceries as I could carry within my ten-pound weight limit, and carrying them slowly home. After a daily grocery run, I would check my mail.

Once a mundane task, checking the mail became quite an adventure. When a package would arrive, I would slowly, cautiously walk down the hall to the package room, pray my box would be less than ten pounds, and carry it back to my apartment. This whole process, once a five-minute ordeal, became a thirty-minute obstacle course.

Our physical bodies are incredible; we can do these routine tasks like grocery shopping and getting our mail every day without much thought or physical or mental effort. I had never realized this before, but now I'll never forget it.

Recovery was a bitch; let's get that straight. After this experience, I gained an entirely new appreciation and respect for all people who have gone through any intensive physical recovery. Whether you are recovering from a sprained ankle or brain surgery, I now empathize greatly with you in a way I never could before.

I also quickly learned that having cancer is essentially like having a birthday celebration you really don't want every single day. Each day, I received cards and gifts in the mail. Truly thoughtful, but honestly somewhat depressing after I realized these gifts were essentially saying, "*Stay alive! You can do it!*"

Most days for the first two weeks after surgery, I was so tired I had to be sitting or lying down at all times. When I did push myself to get up, my walking speed was the speed I used to silently but aggressively judge others for while angrily wondering why they had nothing better to do than walk at a snail's pace all day.

Now, I was the snail. It was hard to be the snail.

As a slow snail, however, I found myself appreciating the little joys of each day more than before. Breakfast became a delicious thirty-minute pleasure. Taking a hot shower on my own two feet felt like standing under the clouds of heaven and feeling magic rain down around me. Drinking a mug of hot, black aromatic coffee with my own hands and the ability to swallow became something I will never again take for granted. I realized that these small, precious, snail-like moments might just be some of the best ones we have in this wild life. That day I decided that it's OK to be the snail; sometimes we need to crawl slowly to enjoy the path.

A few days later, I woke up, filled with nerves as I headed to my first appointment with the neuro-oncologist. She was a kind, young, and stylish doctor. She wore red lipstick and sassy black heels. I liked her immediately.

Dr. Lenn* sat down next to me and asked how much I wanted to know about the pathology results. I explained to Dr. Lenn that although I am a physician, I am not a neurologist or an oncologist, so I wanted to hear the results in a way a layperson would understand.

Dr. Lenn smiled softly and began to tell me about my cancer. As an internal medicine physician, I mostly treat patients with diabetes, heart failure, kidney failure, lung disease, high blood pressure, and heart attacks. I treat patients with cancer too, but only with the help of an oncologist. This information was as new and surprising to me as it would be to you.

The doctor said calmly, "You have a glioma. To be more specific, you have a grade two or three glioma. This is not benign. Brain cancer is not described in stages like other cancers are. Brain cancer is defined in grades. Brain cancer can be grade one to grade four. Grade one only happens in children; it is benign and can be cured by surgery. Grade two and grade three gliomas are also called astrocytomas and are more aggressive. Grade four brain cancer is known as glioblastoma. As you likely know, a glioblastoma is an incredibly aggressive cancer."

With this, my heart started to race. In medicine, a glioblastoma is known as "the terminator" of cancers. It is a universally aggressive, fatal cancer that often kills its victims within months regardless of treatment. I can almost guarantee that if you ask any physician what type of cancer he or she would least like to be diagnosed with, it will be glioblastoma or pancreatic cancer, both of which are deadly, understudied, and almost always discovered too late.

Dr. Lenn went on, "Fortunately, your pathology did not show a glioblastoma." My heart rate slowed a bit.

"However," she cautioned, "grade two and three gliomas are not curable. Glioblastomas, being the most aggressive and deadly, are becoming more researched. Grade two and three gliomas, unfortunately, are underfunded and under-researched. As far as we know, they all progress someday to secondary glioblastoma, regardless of how they are treated. We don't know how long this transformation takes, but it seems to happen in all cases eventually."

I tried to take in this information. In a way, Dr. Lenn was telling me what I would die from, but not when I would die from it. I had just received a death sentence with the date set as *TBD*. She went on, "Low-grade gliomas can sometimes remain stable for ten years before they start to progress. Unfortunately, we don't know if your tumor has been growing in your brain for one year or for eight years."

Can you imagine getting this type of information? I had a

deadly bomb sitting in my brain. A bomb that had been there potentially for years, lurking quietly until it could find the opportune moment to scare me. I would bet money that I graduated from medical school with a brain tumor and hiked Doi Suthep mountain with a brain tumor. How much of my personality, my decisions, had been influenced by this tumor? I would never know.

"What now?" I asked nervously.

Dr. Lenn replied, "We treat gliomas with surgery, chemotherapy, and radiation to try to keep them stable as long as we can, potentially years. Luckily, in your case, we think your glioma is low grade, meaning you may not need treatment besides surgery for a long time."

Dr. Lenn was not talking about the surgery I'd just had, which was a biopsy, a simple diagnostic procedure. She was talking about a second, more invasive surgery, one designed to excise as much of the tumor as possible. She said she would call me after my next appointment with Dr. Clair to discuss surgery details the following week.

Brace yourself, I thought. *This ride is just beginning.*

19

Who says you can't cry at the gym?

"The best thing for being sad," replied Merlin . . . "is to learn something. That's the only thing that never fails."

—T. H. White

I had been told what I will likely die from, but not when I will die from it. I had no time to think, *Would I want to know what I will die from? Would it make things better or worse?* And once I had this information, it become impossible *not* to think about it.

I started to wonder if perhaps I only thought I had the correct information. As a type-A, somewhat neurotic life planner, I had always wondered if I would want this much information. Now I had been given a more detailed guidebook to my life and my death than most people will ever get. The trouble is, things change, and a guidebook is not ideal when every event is proceeded by "maybe" or "if this happens, then perhaps this will happen." Most likely, brain cancer will be the thing that kills me someday. But then again, maybe it won't be.

I was diagnosed with a vague and unsettling type of brain cancer that can kill me whenever it sees fit. I will live with this cancer until I die, either from it or, if I'm incredibly unlucky, from something else beforehand. This type of brain cancer is not something that can be completely surgically removed. It is not always treated with a certain type of chemotherapy or radiation. It is rare and understudied. I like to be unique, but this is more than I bargained for.

Some people live with this type of cancer for many years with relatively few symptoms. The problem is, no one knows how long I have had this cancer. Have I had it for one year or twenty? If it's been there for one, I could be in luck and live a long, relatively unchanged life. If it's been there for twenty, hell, this year could be my last.

When I thought about this, it brought up a few realizations. First, we are all dying from something, even if we don't know what it is yet. Second, none of us know how long we have left to live, yet we live our lives expecting many more years to come. Should we be living this way? Or should all of us, whether we've been told it or not, live as though this year could be our last? I've started to think the second way is best.

Perhaps I was given the most incredible gift. I can live each day, each year, as if it is my last one. If time keeps coming, great! If not, at least I will have lived each moment as the best moment of my entire life. In some ways, I now believe my diagnosis was the greatest, most difficult, most life-changing gift I've ever received.

Prior to my time in Thailand, I had been on an exercise kick. I was not only practicing yoga but getting into some new exercise routines including deadlifting. The week I left for Thailand, I was literally in the very best physical shape of my life, yet now I found myself unable to walk more than fifteen minutes at a time. I needed to use a shower chair while washing my hair. Oh, the cruel irony!

I returned to the gym on day six of surgical recovery to take a slow walk on the treadmill. I found myself nervous about running into my deadlifting buddies since I would have to decrease my weight lifting from the 150-pound barbells I'd been lifting to the 4-pound hand weights of a strange postsurgical reality.

It took me over an hour to change into my workout clothes, tie my shoes without falling over, fill my water bottle, and get on the treadmill. I walked at two miles per hour for forty-five minutes and lifted four-pound weights for a very small number of reps. I had never in my entire life been prouder of anything I had ever done. I crushed that fucking workout. Naturally, I bought myself a postworkout smoothie.

After my successful exercise, I decided to stop in the gym manager's office to request extra guest passes. Since I was still slow and unsteady on my feet, I figured going to the gym with a buddy for a few weeks might be a safe idea. I walked confidently into the manager's office ready to explain my unique situation. I told one manager, then another, and finally a third. As each looked at me with confusion, I began to feel frustrated. No one seemed to understand my request.

Part of the problem was that I looked normal. I wore fashionable gym clothes, spoke normally, walked normally, and my neurosurgeons had managed to operate on me without cutting significant amounts of my hair. At the end of my third retelling of my strange, sad story, the manager looked at me and asked, "So who is the surgical patient that you want to get guest passes for?"

Me, you moron, I thought—hopefully I said something nicer aloud. Once the manager finally realized that I was indeed the person who had recently undergone brain surgery, I received a look of shock and awe. Slightly embarrassed, he tried to backtrack. He asked, "When was your surgery? They didn't shave your head? Wow, you look great for being one week out of surgery." I smiled awkwardly, unsure of what to say.

The manager started to compare surgical stories with me. He was friendly and trying to be relatable by saying things like, "When I had heart surgery, I remember how hard it was to have a weight limit." He started to ask me specific details: "How long will you have a weight limit? When will you be able to get back into deadlifting?" He meant well, but as his questions went on, I realized how few of them I could answer.

My limitations, it occurred to me, were not necessarily related to surgery. Instead, they would depend on the speed at which my cancer decided to kill me, to take away my ability to balance, walk, speak, and think.

Looking at the ground, tears filled my eyes. I tried hard to be emotionless, but I could not hold the flood back. I looked up at him, openly sobbing. "Sir, I have brain cancer. I do not know the answers to these questions. I would like some extra guest passes, so I can enjoy exercising with friends for as long as I can." Looking back, I realize that this was the first time I had to tell a stranger I had cancer. This was the first time I had to publicly admit I was not normal and never would be again.

I'm sorry for the shock I caused this manager, whom I left speechless. I walked away with unlimited guest passes and stopped crying after I bought myself a new book and a brownie. Brain cancer does have some perks, after all.

That day I learned it's OK to cry at the gym. Also, a new book and a brownie may just have magical healing powers themselves.

20

Why be the bird when you can be the whole sky?

One of the best descriptions of awareness comes from Chögyam Trungpa Rinpoche. In a class he was teaching he drew a loose V shape in the center of a large white sheet of paper. "What is this a picture of?" he asked. The students all responded, "It's a bird." "No," Trungpa Rinpoche said. "It's a picture of the sky, with a bird flying through it." Like the sky, awareness is open and spacious. If we focus on this spaciousness rather than on any particular thought or feeling arising in it, we are free.

—Sharon Salzberg

Shortly after my marital separation, a month before I left for Thailand, I had received a gift in the mail from my aunt. This gift was a book entitled *Faith,* written by Sharon Salzberg. Salzberg is an author, meditation instructor, and cofounder of the Insight Meditation Society and the Barre Center for Buddhist Studies in Barre, Massachusetts. She is a fantastic spiritual teacher.

When *Faith* arrived in the mail, I was slightly shocked and felt uncomfortable. Although spiritual in many ways, I did not consider myself a religious person and wondered what sort of cryptic self-help message my aunt was trying to send me. I decided I had faith in her judgment, even if I remained skeptical about the title, so I sat down next to a full pot of coffee and paged through this puzzling book.

I read *Faith* from cover to cover in about an hour. I smiled, I cried, I underlined more passages than I could count. There were repeated pauses as I looked up from the pages and yelled at myself for judging a book simply because I didn't like the title or the self-imposed biases associated with the topic.

Over time, I've come to champion the idea that religion exists as a way to bring us all comfort, community, love, and compassion. I do not think one religion is the correct one, or that anyone's religious beliefs should be changed. As long as your own unique spiritual, religious, agnostic, magical, or devious beliefs encourage you to have a kind heart as well as love and compassion for yourself and others, I think your beliefs are valid. For me, opening my mind to thinking that every belief could be correct instead of thinking that no belief or only one belief is correct gave me incredible peace.

When I first read the passage quoted at the start of this chapter after my marital separation, it gave me strength and courage. It made me think, *Maybe marriage isn't the bird in the center of my life; maybe it is simply a bird flying through a vast life I have left to live.*

Postsurgery, I reread this passage and thought, *Maybe cancer is not the bird in the center of my life either. Maybe it is simply a small mark on the canvas of a vast life I have left to live.*

Why focus on being the bird when I can be the whole sky?

21

Badass new boots

This moving away from comfort and security, this
stepping out into what is unknown, uncharted,
and shaky—that's called liberation.

—Pema Chödrön

After my unexpected public meltdown at the gym, I walked a block down the street to a bookstore. This was actually the same bookstore where *The Universe in a Single Atom* had fallen and hit me on the head a few fateful months ago. I strolled back to the Buddhist literature section, still crying, and found another book written by my dream pal, the Dalai Lama. I bought *An Open Heart: Practicing Compassion in Everyday Life* and walked to the bus stop a block away. At a few weeks postsurgery, it was not yet safe for me to drive.

Sitting down on the bus, trying to slow my last few tears, I started reading. I read this book all the way back to my apartment, then made a slow trek up to my couch, where I continued to read. I devoured the entire thing, loving every page.

And yet, even though this book was a beautiful summary of how to have compassion and wisdom in our everyday lives, when I'd finished, I found myself sulking. My mind was telling me, *Poor you, you have cancer. Poor you, you only have a few years left to live. Poor you, no one understands your story.* These thoughts continued in a circle of endless negativity until I felt suffocated.

But then, I got a message. A package had arrived for me in my apartment's delivery room. After a slow walk downstairs, I returned to my apartment with a large box. Opening it, I found the most badass new boots I've ever seen. "Thank you, genius Courtney," I told myself. "Thank you for ordering these amazingly badass new boots. You forgot you even ordered them, but you need them now more than ever before."

I had never been so excited to put on a pair of new boots. These were sturdy, rugged, combat-style boots like nothing I had ever worn before. Slipping them on my feet, I felt like a new person.

Suddenly, the lessons the Dalai Lama had been trying to tell me kicked in. It was as if these badass new boots held the wisdom of the world in their beautiful soles. I had been looking at the negative side of things all day long. Now I had badass new boots on my feet, and I was alive to see another day. Why had I been so upset?

I kept my new boots on and left my apartment, thinking, *Complaining won't change a thing, but it will make my precious time less happy and less fulfilling.* As any faithful Buddhist practitioner will tell you, everything is impermanent. Instead of fearing impermanence, I decided to embrace it.

Feelings of sadness, of hopelessness, of unfairness—these are impermanent. Health, youth, naivete—these, unfortunately, are impermanent too. The wisdom of impermanence brings us an understanding that everything will change. To find happiness and acceptance, we have to enjoy the good moments while we are living them. None of these moments will last forever. The important thing is to experience them fully when they are here.

22

Meet Monsieur

Is there anything I can do to make myself enlightened?
As little as you can do to make the sun rise in the morning.
Then of what use are the spiritual exercises you prescribe?
To make sure you are not asleep when the sun begins to rise.

—Anthony De Mello

In the midst of recovery, as I tried to keep my blog updated with thoughtful, funny, and inspiring posts, there were a few days I found myself simply too exhausted to write. My mother made a few guest appearances in my absence, sharing stories she had written from her perspective on this unexpected and difficult journey.

I come from a long line of writers and storytellers, and I owe credit to these amazing ladies for passing along some of their gifts. My mother always told me she thought she would be a writer—her mother, my grandmother, was a published author—but she never found she had anything to say. The abrupt shift in my life trajectory changed that. She found that sleepless nights spent worrying about my condition were better spent formulating thoughts about this unexpected situation.

One day, my mother emailed me a story she had typed up. I started to read her words: "Reading to my children was one of my greatest pleasures in early motherhood. What a win/win situation—the warmth of a content child on one's lap, the quiet transition to nap or bedtime, and the hope that one is transforming the little one into a reader—this is all good stuff."

I started to tear up and continued reading. "Courtney's brain has always been busy. One night, around age four, she was lying in bed next to me chatting about this or that when she started telling me about Monsieur. I asked who she was talking about, and she tapped the side of her head and said, 'You know. In here!' It took me a minute to realize that Courtney was talking about her brain."

I called my mom, laughing and crying at this strange story. "Is this true, Mom?" I asked her.

I had named my brain. How bizarre. I didn't speak French; my mother and father don't speak French. To this day, my mother will still tell you she has no idea where I learned that word.

Although I was too drugged after surgery to remember, my mother told me she spoke quietly to Monsieur before my first brain surgery. She says, "I told Monsieur to figure out a way to get rid of the bad parts and keep the good parts. I would like to think Monsieur is working hard on this project." Mom, I hope so too.

Monsieur, you crazy lunatic, you better be doing the right thing in there.

23

I am the lucky one

No matter how long we live, at most around a hundred years, eventually we must die, losing this valuable human life. And it could happen at any time. This life will disintegrate, no matter how much prosperity we have. No amount of wealth can buy an extension on your life.

—the Dalai Lama

Over the past few years of my career as an internal medicine resident, I have seen many patients. Every patient's story stays with me in some way. Some bring me happiness, some sadness, some joy, some guilt. They all teach me as much as or more than I can ever hope to teach them.

My initial career dream was to be a teacher. I worked as a tutor for many years, teaching both local and international students in science, math, and college test preparation.

In college, I majored in genetics. Teaching was still my passion—I actually contemplated pursuing a PhD rather than an MD in order to start a career as a genetics professor. However, I was also interested in medicine. I volunteered at a number of hospitals, nursing homes, and clinics to experience caring for patients. I soon learned that the medical field allows endless teaching opportunities, in addition to endless learning opportunities. In medicine, I could learn the stories of many patients. Through their stories, they inspired me.

As I wrote my blog, I received unexpectedly amazing, kind

comments from many readers. These comments made me realize that I had been given a very unique gift. Although the outside of the gift said "brain cancer," inside I found an opportunity to teach people in a completely different and unexpected way.

Prior to my own diagnosis and transition from physician to patient, I often saw patients who were dying. Young patients, in particular, affected me deeply, as their deaths were usually the toughest to witness.

As a new resident physician, I met a thirty-year-old man with metastatic lung cancer. He was dying. His hospital room was filled with flowers, photos, and family members at all times. His last wish was for his two golden retrievers to visit him in the hospital. We snuck the dogs in, they snuggled with him, and he died the following morning. All I could think was, *This is so unfair. This poor man was so young. He was newly married. He must have been so sad and scared to die.*

Later that year, I worked with a twenty-five-year-old woman who had liver failure. New diagnosis, horrible prognosis. She needed a new liver and would never get one. My thoughts were, *This is so unfair. This poor girl. Why is this happening to her? She must be so sad and scared to die.*

A few months before Thailand, I worked with a thirty-year-old man with metastatic melanoma. His hospital room was also filled with flowers, photos, and family. He was dying, quickly. Every time I went into his room I thought, *This is so unfair. Why does this young man have this horrible disease? He must be so sad and scared to die.*

I could go on and on here. I have seen many cases very similar to these. Unfortunately, illness and death are not uncommon, even in the young.

You might wonder, "Why are you telling me these sad stories? I don't want to read about death." I tell you these stories because I realize now, as a patient, that I may have misinterpreted every one of them. I looked at these patients, talked to these patients, and walked away thinking, *They must be so sad, so upset at how unfair life has been to them; they must be so scared to die.* If you have lost a loved one and had these thoughts, I want to reassure you that they are not always the thoughts a patient has at all.

After I was diagnosed with terminal brain cancer at twenty-nine years old, I realized, *I am actually the lucky one.* Let me explain why.

Ever since my diagnosis, my greatest sadness comes from thinking about the sadness my family and friends will have to experience when I die. I assume many young patients diagnosed with a terminal illness feel the same way. It's a terrible thought to know that my parents, my brother, my friends will have to experience suffering and heartbreak due to my illness and eventual death, which will very likely occur before their own.

As a person facing her own mortality, however, I've realized I will not have to experience this same heartbreak. I will die, but I will not have to live without people that I love. Because of this, I am the lucky one.

24

Brain surgery. Sure, let's do it again.

May we realize that there is no time to waste,
Death being definite but the time of death indefinite.
What has gathered will separate, what has been
accumulated will be consumed without residue,
At the end of a rising comes descent,
the finality of birth is death.

—First Panchen Lama, stanza three of a poem
many Tibetans use when reflecting on dying

During week three of surgical recovery, I had a repeat MRI scan followed by a meeting with Dr. Clair to determine next steps in my treatment plan. I was incredibly nervous. There was a small chance this scan would show that the remaining tumor was inoperable, situated in a position too risky to excavate. This would mean I needed immediate chemotherapy and radiation instead.

Fortunately, I received great news. Dr. Clair told me my remaining tumor was operable. I would get to have a second, more invasive surgery in two weeks. I met up with my parents for dinner after the appointment to celebrate, and we all laughed at how our perspectives had changed over the past few weeks. "Another brain surgery? Sure, let's do it," I said as we cheered over chilled chardonnay and mutual fear.

Although this was "great" news, I knew surgery was not a curative treatment. As I mentioned, I was diagnosed with a type of cancer that unfortunately cannot be cured with surgery, or anything. The purpose of this second surgery was to prevent the tumor from growing rapidly or causing symptoms, and hopefully lengthen my life in the process. Regardless, I knew I would live with this cancer as a chronic disease for the rest my life. I accepted this. As Buddha reportedly said, "Though you hold fast, you cannot stay. What benefit is there in being frightened and scared of what is unalterable?"

You cannot stay. I cannot stay. It's beautiful in its profoundly accurate simplicity. The finality of birth is death. This is something we know with complete certainty but often fail to accept.

> *Always know that life is beautiful and you have only one life to live . . . You live what you think and feel all day and it is in your very own hands to make your little heaven on this earth. Life is beautiful; do not complicate it.*

—Mridula Agarwal, *The 10 Rules of Happiness*

꧁

Three weeks after my first surgery and one month before my second, I celebrated by going back to work full time. My residency program was nothing but supportive of me during recovery. I was not forced to return to work, but I chose to—I love what I do, and it turns out I am terrible at relaxing.

I have never been more excited to go to work on a Monday morning than I was that day. On my way to the parking garage, I heard three different people complain about "Monday morning." Prior to this, I would have been right there with them. Now, all I could think was, *What is there to complain about? It's a beautiful, sunny Monday morning. We are walking to our nice cars in our comfortable and convenient parking garage in our fancy apartment complex to drive to our paying jobs. We are healthy enough to work. We are not stuck in bed today. This is a day that should be celebrated.* Looking back now, mid-pandemic, I find this even more relevant.

This was the first and likely only morning I have ever thought about how much time I usually spend complaining about mornings. I smiled, sipped my fancy coffee, and went to work. I told myself that I would not complain about this or any other morning with the knowledge that in one month, my mornings would again consist of recovering from a craniotomy.

I knew these future mornings would involve me sitting in a dark room in bed, unable to stand for more than sixty seconds at a time, unable to walk at more than a snail's pace, unable to have the television or music or lights on, unable to hold a conversation for more than a few minutes at a time. Anticipating the suffering to come made this sunny, normal Monday seem surprisingly wonderful and joyful.

I was scheduled to work in a primary care clinic that week. My clinic director told me I would see patients in the morning but would have the afternoon off to rest. At first, I thought, *Why would I need the afternoon off? I'm feeling great!* However, by noon, I was more exhausted than I had ever been. Despite this, the morning was successful. I met wonderful new patients and felt like I was back in my element.

I took a short nap. When I woke up, I felt every emotion. I was proud of myself for going back to work only three weeks after brain surgery. I was happy I hadn't lost my knowledge and was still able to successfully help patients with a variety of concerns. But I was also profoundly sad. I think the best way to explain this sadness is simply to say that it was emotionally draining to simultaneously feel *in my element* and realize that nothing would ever be the same again.

Multiple patients came in to clinic to discuss new aches and pains. Pain in his back, pain in her knee. After some reassurance, two of my patients made comments along the lines of, "Well, thank God it's not cancer. That would be so much worse." I smiled and nodded, glad they felt better after our discussion. I did not know what to say. On the outside, I looked like their doctor, young, healthy, full of life. On the inside, I knew I was dying, likely faster than the seventy-year-old man sitting in front of me, complaining about the awful pains that come along with age. My mind thought, for just a second, *How wonderful would it be to experience the pains of old age? The beauty of a wrinkle, a gray hair? I would give anything to live long enough to complain about these things.* I knew better than to say these words aloud. I nodded and smiled empathetically, reassuring him before he left.

25

Comrade-in-arms

*The sky was there before the clouds gathered, and it
will be after they have gone. It is also present when the
clouds seem to cover every inch of the sky we can see.*

—the Dalai Lama

Later that week, I worked my first full day in clinic. I made it from
8:00 a.m. to 4:00 p.m., feeling nothing short of complete exhaustion. I now accepted that nothing would ever be the same, but I
felt this in a more positive light. Everything would be different,
but different can be beautiful.

I found myself better equipped to empathize with my patients,
to reassure them and to guide them in matters I was previously
unable to remotely understand. With some patients, I shared my
own story of being a patient. Rather than my experience scaring
them or making them distrust my medical skills as I had feared, I
found they were grateful to have a doctor who could fully understand what they were going through: what it felt like to be sick, to
be scared, to be labeled with a new diagnosis, to start a new medication, to experience an abrupt change in plans. I found myself
granted a new privilege. Not only was I still a physician and an
educator, I was also a comrade-in-arms.

After my first week back at work, I thanked the universe profusely that my brain tumor was not in a location that affected my
thinking, my function, or my ability to practice medicine.

That week, my career plans changed rather abruptly. Instead

of a career in hospital medicine, I decided that I would apply for a job as a primary care physician after my year as chief resident. I like the idea of patients thinking of me as "their doctor," of forming a professional relationship spanning months or, if I'm lucky, even years. Perhaps I will even try to work primarily with young patients with cancer and chronic disease, offering them a unique perspective as both physician and fellow warrior.

The difficult gift of brain cancer kept on giving. It not only inspired me to write, to think critically, and to find happiness despite suffering; it also gave me the gift of being a better, more relatable physician through being a patient as well.

26

Extra-large courage

When we get entangled in a difficult situation ... we must
generate courage equal to the size of the difficulties we face.

—the Dalai Lama

The second week back at work following my first brain surgery
was an interesting one, as I began to catch up with colleagues I
had not seen in quite some time. Some were familiar with my recent diagnosis from my blog. Others were less familiar but knew I
had been diagnosed with *something*. Many seemed nervous to talk
to me, as if they didn't know what to say. A few seemed to have
no idea anything was different in my life. This was refreshing, but
also odd. I felt like a new person inside, even though my exterior
appeared unchanged.

One thing I found intriguing was the incredible variety of reactions people gave me. I would tell two people the exact same story,
yet I would often receive two very unique reactions. I never knew
exactly what to expect, which was both thrilling and exhausting.

Colleagues and friends asked me a fascinating variety of questions that week. Prior to my diagnosis, colleagues used to ask me
questions like, "How are you? How is your dog? How is your work
schedule? Have any fun plans this weekend?" To counter this,
here are a few of the questions colleagues asked me that week:
Are you back at work full time? Why didn't they shave your head
during surgery? Do you feel different? How is your family han-
dling this? Are you actually a Buddhist? What is the pathology

of your tumor? What is your prognosis? Have you looked up any research studies on your treatment plan? Will they need to shave more of your head for the next surgery? Did you actually get divorced? (I had almost forgotten about my divorce at that point.) What medications are you on?

The list could go on. Now, I didn't mind these questions and actually found it somewhat sweet that my colleagues cared so much. However, you can imagine that the first list took slightly less time and energy to answer than the second list.

Therefore, social gatherings left me exhausted. Not only had I returned to work, I had also entered a different social world than I was living in before.

While reflecting on the Dalai Lama's advice to generate courage equal to the size of the difficulties we face, I realized I was facing an extra-large difficulty at that moment. I was a resident physician with cancer working full time; I was recovering from a partial craniotomy; I had a new cancer diagnosis; I was mentally preparing for a second craniotomy; I was going through a divorce. All that, and I wasn't even aware of COVID-19's imminent arrival.

I decided in that moment and in every moment thereafter that I must generate an extra-large amount of courage to overcome extra-large difficulties.

I believe one way to expand courage is to share my own happiness, love, and compassion with others. Buddhist philosophy tells us that we can give away our own happiness using love; similarly, we can take away others' suffering using compassion.

There are many books written about this topic by teachers who have studied this subtle philosophy for many years. I will not pretend I am qualified to write an instruction manual on how to be a Buddhist or how to interpret this advice. However, I will attempt to summarize a powerful idea that I have used to create courage in my own life.

The Dalai Lama states that when we give away our own

happiness and use compassion to help relieve others' suffering, this mental imagery can "increase determination and willpower, while creating a peaceful atmosphere."

When we experience personal misfortune, such as illness, Buddhists are advised to take their suffering and use it to serve as a substitute for the suffering of all other sentient beings. By expanding your perspective to include the suffering of all other beings and by using your own misfortune as a mental trade-off for the suffering of others, your own sorrow will diminish as your courage simultaneously increases.

In summary, I thought: Be kind, be happy. Be compassionate toward others. Share your kindness, love, happiness, and compassion with everyone. Let your own illness or misfortune serve to benefit others and relieve them of their own suffering, expanding your courage through the process. I hope I'm doing this, every day.

27

The old man in the little pink hat

Imagine a boat of desperate refugees crossing the ocean. The boat gets caught in a storm and everyone panics. If everyone panics, there's a high chance they will do the wrong thing and the boat will capsize. But if just one single person can remain calm, they will be able to inspire others to be calm. If, from a place of peace, they ask everyone to sit quietly, the whole boat can be saved. That person doesn't exactly do anything. What they contribute above all is their calmness and the quality of their being.

—Thich Nhat Hanh

I was asked a very interesting question one day by my therapist. She asked, "Do you ever wake up having forgotten you have cancer and feel sad when you remember?"

Have you ever felt this? I recall feeling this during times of heartbreak. After a breakup with an old boyfriend, I can recall mornings waking up with a brief moment of happiness until the heartbreak came rushing back. Interestingly, I never felt this with my cancer diagnosis. In the six weeks that had passed, I would wake up each morning feeling like myself and smiling.

"It's OK to be sad sometimes. You don't have to pretend to be happy," I remember multiple friends telling me. "I'm not pretending," was always my answer, but I could tell they didn't always believe me. *How can this be?* they would wonder.

I think my ability to be happy in the face of suffering was due to many factors, including some of my previous experiences with my own patients. Two patients I worked with have imprinted themselves in my memory forever. When I think about why these two patients stand out, it's the way they generated an uncanny ability to face their own suffering with acceptance and even joy. This is not what I expect of my patients; I am prepared for tears, for sadness, for anger. I am rarely prepared for joy, yet when it happens, it has a profound effect not only on the physician but on every single person the patient interacts with. I want to share these patients' stories with you so you can have a better idea of why, when I channel the energy they embodied, I am able to find the gift within the difficulty.

Patient 1: The old man in the little pink hat

While I was on the oncology service in Thailand, I occasionally left the clinic to work in the hospital itself. Many of its wards, blocks of hospital beds shared by patients who needed similar types of care, were multi-bed wards. This meant that many rows of beds were lined up next to one another in a large room. Our team of ten physicians would walk as a group and stop in front of each patient's bed, discuss their diagnosis, and give them an update on the treatment plan for the day. You can imagine that this could be quite intimidating for a patient.

One morning, I was rounding with the oncology team when I met a patient I will never forget. This man sat in the last bed of the ward. Our team had already stopped to talk with over twenty patients in the same room, all with cancer diagnoses of some sort. All these patients looked sad, tired, confused, and scared. I felt helpless as I met one after another, unable to offer them much hope. But then, I met the old man in the little pink hat.

Imagine the cutest, sweetest old man you've ever seen. This man had cancer. His physical body was dying, and he knew this. Unlike the other patients in his ward who were lying in bed, sleeping, crying, or moaning in pain, this man was sitting cross-legged on the end of his bed, wearing a small, knitted, hot-pink hat. He smiled a huge, toothless smile as we approached the foot of his bed. I have never seen someone look happier than this man. Standing in front of him, I smiled back. I felt happy, optimistic. His mood changed my mood and the mood of the entire medical team.

When I was diagnosed with a brain tumor a month later, I sat in my own hospital bed in Thailand. At first, I felt scared. I felt sad. But then, for some reason, a vivid memory of the old man in the little pink hat flashed in my mind and I felt a wave of overwhelming happiness. I silently thanked this man for giving me relief at the most difficult moment of my life simply by being his calm, peaceful, and happy self. Every time I have gone to my own medical appointments since then, I think of the old man in the little pink hat. I think of his smile, his peaceful presence, and the monk in the saffron robe telling me, "Smile. Do not cry. Find happiness and spread it to the people around you." These thoughts are my keys to happiness.

Patient 2: The man with the forever smile

A few years ago, I was working as a medical student in Chicago at a nursing home. I was instructed to talk with a patient who had lived in the nursing home for the past year.

This patient had a very sad story. He had suffered a traumatic brain injury. Interestingly, this patient's brain injury had altered his personality so that he was constantly happy and smiling. I honestly can't explain this medically and would need to consult a traumatic brain injury specialist to understand fully. As far as I am aware, this is not a common result of traumatic brain injuries.

This patient smiled 100 percent of the time following his injury. I asked the physician I was working with if the patient had a neurologic injury that caused his facial muscles to form a continuous smile. She said no. Somehow, in an almost inexplicable way, this patient had suffered an injury to part of his brain that led to a true personality change. Sometimes this can happen with frontal lobe injuries, but this is a very extreme and rare example. The physician had worked with the same patient before his injury. "This man was often cranky and irritable," she told me. "After his injury, he has smiled constantly and is always happy. Everything makes him happy. Meeting new people, talking to his physicians, eating food, watching television, playing cards, sitting in his wheelchair, even just lying in bed."

I sat and talked with this patient for an hour. The entire time, he smiled. I walked away from him thinking, *If I ever have a brain injury, I hope it's exactly like this. I hope it makes me permanently happy.* You really can't make these stories up.

One morning, around a week before my second brain surgery, I woke up early and read an entire book. I couldn't stop. It was so simple, so beautiful, so well written. This book was *The Art of Living* by Thich Nhat Hanh. Sean actually lent it to me after our return from Thailand.

In this book, Thich Nhat Hanh describes the notion of "non-action." Non-action is the idea that not doing anything is sometimes actually the best thing we can do. The quote I referenced at the beginning of this chapter influenced me deeply in the weeks after my diagnosis.

Many people have asked me why I seem so calm. They have said, "It's OK to be sad. Don't fake a smile." They have asked, "Are you actually OK with all this, or are you just putting on a good face? Express your emotions. Don't act happy just for our sake."

Every time I hear these comments, I tell my friends and family that my attitude about my diagnosis is not fake. I am not upset. I am not mad. I do not wake up and think this is just a bad dream.

I am truly calm. I am truly happy. I am at peace. We can't predict or prepare for the challenges life throws at us, but we can choose how we respond to them.

I think of the old man in the little pink hat and the forever happy man, and I can relate. I read Thich Nhat Hanh's words, and I can relate.

Despite the storm, I choose to be the calm passenger on the boat. There is no need to panic. Panic will only lead to the boat capsizing. Calmness, peace, and acceptance are the qualities I use to keep my boat afloat.

28

This is our moment

We have to make this present moment into the
most wonderful moment of our life.

—Thich Nhat Hanh

I recently learned how important it is to be present, to be mindful of what is happening right *now*. In this moment. The past is gone, the future is not promised. We are only guaranteed this exact moment, precisely as it is.

I used to spend so much time worrying about the future. Will I get into medical school? Will I get into a residency program? Will I get married? When will my next vacation be? Will I get a job? Will my husband, friends, coworkers still like me next month, or will they be sick of me? Have I made enough plans for this evening, this weekend? The list could go on infinitely.

Then, I went to Thailand. Each day was a new, exciting day. I had no idea what to expect from moment to moment. One day, I was meeting new patients in a hospital in Chiang Mai. The next day, I was hiking up a mountain, stumbling onto majestic hidden temples with a new friend. Later, I was sitting in an old, red, rusty songthaew, heading to an unknown city to volunteer with sick rescued elephants. Next, I was getting a Thai massage in the nicest spa I've ever seen. One day, I started to have seizures, but then I felt fine and met friends from all over the world at yoga class. After this, I was on a dinner date eating delicious coconut curry. Not more than one week later, I found myself lying in a hospital bed in Minnesota recovering from brain surgery. Shortly after this, a neurosurgeon told me I had brain cancer.

Life is funny. If you had asked my previously high-strung, overly controlling self what was on my January–February 2020 schedule, I would not have meticulously written down any of the things I just told you in my daily planner.

I learned a valuable lesson throughout all this. In this moment and in all moments to come, I hope I can remind myself to stay present. To think about how much I have *right now.*

How much we hope to have, or plan to have, or expect to have in the upcoming months or years is not guaranteed to any of us. We have only this moment. We are breathing; we are living; we are exactly where we are supposed to be.

My simple advice is this. Plan a little, but don't plan too much. This exact moment is the only moment you're absolutely guaranteed to have. Look around—see how beautiful it is?

29

COVID-19, cancer, craziness

Happiness is a state of mind. With physical comforts if your mind is still in a state of confusion and agitation, it is not happiness. Happiness means calmness of mind.

—the Dalai Lama

On March 11, 2020, the WHO declared COVID-19 a pandemic. Due to the recommendation for social distancing and the rapid spread of virus throughout my community, I began to work remotely, practicing telemedicine in a virtual pandemic unit where I counseled patients who had been exposed to or developed symptoms of the virus. I often found myself feeling frustrated that in the two weeks prior to my next brain surgery, I had to practice social distancing. I could not travel, could not eat at my favorite restaurants, could not see my family or friends.

Instead, all I could do was use my unexpected time alone to try to appreciate the small miracles of the present moment. There is a famous quote, attributed by some to Albert Einstein, that says, "There are two ways to live your life. One is as though nothing is a miracle. The other is as though everything is a miracle."

Max, whom I briefly dated in Thailand, kept in touch with me after my diagnosis. He mentioned one day that he thought I might be in denial about my cancer diagnosis because he didn't understand how I could come to terms with my own mortality so quickly. He was shocked when I said I was calm and at peace with the knowledge that my life span is more limited than initially thought. He asked me, "How can such a young person be OK with the idea of dying? It doesn't seem normal."

I answered this question in three ways. First, I am a physician. I speak to people about death every day. I have witnessed death many times. None of this is to say that I minimize death, but I do feel that death is a natural part of life. Medicine cannot prevent it. Science cannot prevent it. Why fear something we cannot change?

Second, I practice Buddhism. As my favorite life coach, the Dalai Lama, states, "If you accept that death is part of life, then when it actually does come, you may face it more easily."

Third, facing my own mortality has been a difficult, yet wonderful, gift. I now look at each moment with fresh eyes. I am thankful for ordinary moments that I once took for granted.

Max did not seem to like this answer. He asked, "Why aren't you more hopeful for a miracle that you will be cured?"

Statistically, it would be highly unlikely for my cancer to be *cured*. I understand that statistics cannot explain everything, but I also refuse to live my life in ignorance. If I outlive the statistics, I will be grateful. If I do not, I will still be grateful for every precious moment I was allowed to live.

I prefer to believe that everything is a miracle rather than wait for one huge, magical, statistically unlikely miracle to occur. By being aware of my own mortality, I feel more prepared to appreciate each little, mundane moment as its one small miracle.

The real miracles are breathing, eating, walking, talking, smiling, petting my dog, going to work, hugging my family and friends, reading a book, watching a sunset, going to sleep in a comfortable bed in a comfortable home, and waking up to see the sunrise another day.

If we live our lives waiting for huge miracles that will likely never come, isn't this akin to living our lives thinking that nothing is a miracle? Or even worse, missing the many small miracles that happen all the time?

If I continued to live angry at the world, waiting for my cancer to be inexplicably cured, I felt it would be living my life "as though nothing is a miracle." Instead, I choose to live my life believing that everything is a miracle, most importantly the things I used to take for granted.

Today and every day, we can participate in many miraculous moments, including eating a favorite snack with the ability to taste, watching a show on Netflix with eyes that can see and ears that can hear, walking our dogs with bodies that can move, and talking on the phone using technology that makes social distancing not so bad after all.

> *You are not the only person who suffers . . . You may believe that your suffering is greater than anyone else's, or that you are the only person who suffers, but this is not true. When you recognize the suffering around you it will help you to suffer less.*
>
> —Thich Nhat Hanh

༄

Our beautiful, messy world has always been full of uncertainty and suffering. This is not new. Everyone in this world experiences suffering.

During the COVID-19 pandemic, the suffering was more visible than ever before. During frightening times, all of us were constantly reminded of suffering by our own symptoms, by our community as businesses shut their doors, by social media with its constant terrifying updates, and by our isolating situations as we distanced ourselves from others and tried to settle into a new way of living within the walls of our homes.

No better time than in the middle of a global pandemic to have my second brain surgery. My incredible neurosurgery team scheduled me for a craniotomy on Thursday, March 19, 2020, in an attempt to remove more of the astrocytoma invading my brain.

30

Craniotomy round two

When you wake up in the morning, you can choose how
you want to start your day. I recommend you start the
day smiling. Why smile? Because you are alive and
you have twenty-four brand new hours ahead of you.
The new day is a gift of life offered to you. Celebrate
it and vow to live it deeply. Vow not to waste it.

—Thich Nhat Hanh

My second craniotomy was scheduled on a Thursday in March. Due to the ongoing pandemic, visitors were not allowed in the hospital. My poor parents, sick with anxiety about leaving me at the hospital door for such a major procedure, picked me up from my apartment and dropped me off on a chilly, dark morning before dawn. As they hugged me goodbye, I thought of the very surreal experience I was having. Here I found myself, standing outside the hospital where I worked, dropped off by my parents, about to undergo surgery for cancer I hadn't known was living in my brain just two short months ago. As if this scene weren't strange enough, add a global pandemic. There we stood with face masks on, terrified with the rest of the world, but with our own unique fears added on. The cold, starlit predawn sky created an otherworldly experience, enhanced by the presence of stern security guards at the entrance ensuring no one but hospital personnel and patients entered the building.

"Don't worry. It's just another brain surgery," I told my parents as I hugged them goodbye. "Once you've had one, you've had them all. No big deal. I love you." Holding back tears, I stepped forward into the hospital as if to start another day at work.

"Hey guys!" I stopped in the resident workroom and chatted with the medicine residents, dropping off a box of donuts for the team. "Enjoy my hair, this is the last time you might see it," I joked, thinking I was quite hilarious, before taking the staff elevator up to the preoperative area. Checking in, I chatted with the receptionist and nurses, many of whom I had worked with. The lobby was deserted, as all nonessential surgeries were canceled during the pandemic. The waiting room was eerily quiet, the world seeming to stand still.

A nurse brought me a gown to change into, and I got myself situated in a patient bed. I chatted with my nurse, my lab technician, and my surgeons as colleagues, almost forgetting that I was also a patient. I thanked them for the respect they showed me, calling me "doctor" and keeping me updated as if it were just another day at work.

My surgical nurse, Steve, was my hero that day. He entered my room full of energy. His full-sleeve tattoo was fiery, sassy, and bold. I liked him immediately.

"Steve, I think I'm having minor PTSD being back in the operating room after my experiences as a medical student," I joked, not entirely unserious. Medical students are constantly yelled at by surgical nurses when they scrub in incorrectly (and for good reason, as it takes a very specific order of procedures to sterilize oneself before entering a surgical room). My palms were sweating and my heart was racing not because my skull was about to be opened, but because I was having flashbacks to my first surgical rotation as a medical student in urology. I'll never forget Tanya, the surgical nurse who stared me down as I scrubbed into my first urologic surgery, waiting until I was putting on my last glove before yelling, "Stop! Throw it all out and scrub in again; you aren't sterile." Freezing like a lost kid in the grocery store, I followed Tanya's specific instructions, going through two more gowns before I got it right.

"Don't worry," Steve told me, laughing a little, "I won't make you scrub in today. I'll do it for you." He draped a sterile blanket over me and wheeled me into the operating room, where hot, bright lights shone down on me, giving me the impression of a search-and-rescue helicopter shining its lights directly into a drowning swimmer's eyes. *"Down here, we've found her,"* I almost heard Steve say.

Steve laughed at me as I told him about my medical student memories and tried to keep calm. We gossiped, shared funny stories, and traded tips on where to find the best food in the Twin Cities. As the anesthesiologist put the mask on my face to put me to sleep, I requested of Steve, "Write down the name of that restaurant you mentioned so I can get that pesto sandwich after this chaos is over." As Steve smiled and held my hand, I instantly fell asleep.

I woke up around seven hours later in the post-anesthesia care unit, or PACU. Pinned to my gown was a piece of paper (literally, a tag from a surgical sterilization kit) with a restaurant recommendation scribbled on the back of it.

Waking up alone postsurgery was a bizarre experience. To be honest, it felt even more like I was simply at work rather than a patient emerging from brain surgery. I often found myself confused as to my role. I vividly recall hearing a patient across from me in the PACU coughing loudly. Looking at him and his monitors, he appeared to be in respiratory distress due to heart failure. The nurses around me called for the surgical team. "Quick, we need help with bed twelve," they paged overhead.

"Get him a bilevel positive airway pressure machine and forty milligrams of furosemide, stat," I yelled. I saw confused, annoyed eyes from the medical staff glaring back at me, a young woman with a blood-soaked bandage around her head lying in bed yelling out medical advice. Embarrassed, I remembered where I was and pretended I hadn't said a thing, although I knew my advice was right.

After an hour or so, I was wheeled up to a room in the neuro-surgical intensive care unit. Without visitors, it was eerily quiet. I was relieved to find that my ICU nurse was the same nurse who had worked with me after my first surgery. She told me, "We are here for you. We have been thinking of you, and all the nurses are rooting for you." I did not feel I deserved so much love.

Later that evening, Dr. Clair came into my room. "How are you feeling?" he asked. "You did great. We got out nearly all of the tumor, at least 95 percent. A small piece was too close to a major blood vessel for us to safely remove, but overall, it was a tremendous success." As he said this, I noticed he looked somewhat sad. "Have you looked in the mirror yet?" he asked me.

"Not yet," I replied nervously.

Holding up a mirror, I saw that the left side of my face was essentially paralyzed. I could not lift the left corner of my mouth at all; it sat in a permanent frown. I could not blink my left eye closed, and, after lifting a spoon of applesauce to my mouth, I soon learned that I could not eat with the left-sided muscles of my mouth. I looked as though I'd had a stroke.

"You did not have a stroke," Dr. Clair spoke as if reading my mind. "Your peripheral nerves were irritated during surgery. Your facial muscles will recover, but it may take up to six months."

Six months without a full smile? Six months of looking like a patient? I felt like I had been punched. Yet, from somewhere deep within, I heard the monk in Thailand remind me, "*Smile. Do not cry.*"

I gave Dr. Clair my best half smile and told him, "You got out the tumor. I can live for a while without a full smile. It's OK." I got the feeling he was trying to hold back a tear as he thanked me and left the room.

Nightfall came, and I managed to eat a cup of soup, only half of it landing on my shirt. I not only looked like I'd had a stroke, I felt like it too.

I asked my nurse if I could try walking. Nervous to see if my other muscles were functioning, I cautiously got to my feet, stood up, and took a few slow steps. I could walk. I could balance. I reminded myself that I could still talk, still read, still think. *I may look silly for a few months, but I am here and I am alive,* I told myself as I watched my floppy smile attempt to move in the mirror. At that moment, I channeled the old man in the little pink hat and thanked him. I sat calmly, grateful to be alive. Grateful to have even one more day on this beautiful planet, grateful to see the sunrise one more time, grateful to have half a smile.

After another long night of neurologic checks every hour, morning came and two of my fellow residents stopped by to see me. No visitors were allowed, but fortunately hospital workers were an exception. They traded my horrific hospital coffee for a handcrafted latte and didn't say a word about my smile. As I sipped, I felt small drops of coffee leak out of the left side of my mouth. I was a twenty-nine-year-old woman trapped in the body of a ninety-year-old stroke victim. I started to feel sorry for myself, but then I remembered Thich Nhat Hanh's words: "*I recommend you start the day smiling . . . The new day is a gift of life offered to you.*"

I read this quote in the ICU and typed a new blog post that morning. "Hey family and friends, I survived. I may have only half of a smile, but I will use it."

A few hours later, Dr. Clair stopped in and handed me my discharge paperwork. He took ten minutes to sit with me and talk about life; I appreciated this more than he will ever know.

When I walked out of the hospital, my parents were waiting to drive me home. Dr. Clair and I had warned them that my face looked different. My parents put on a brave face and smiled at me, but I could see their fear. "*Spread happiness to the people around you,*" I remembered the monk telling me. With a half smile and a full heart, I hugged them and got in the car to drive home.

31

No mud, no lotus. No resilience, no recovery.

*Changing the way we see the world in turn
changes the way we feel and the way we act . . .
With our mind we create our own world.*

—the Dalai Lama

As I recovered from surgery at my parents' house, I reflected on a few unique personalities I was taking on: that of an immunosuppressed recovering brain cancer patient during a pandemic; that of an overwhelmed and slightly terrified resident physician during a pandemic; that of a novice yet studious Buddhist practitioner trying to spread happiness and relieve the suffering of herself and others; and that of a recently single young woman trying to navigate the dating scene for the first time in her life, not only mid-pandemic but also with a large incision in her skull and a floppy smile. It makes me tired just reflecting on this time of my life.

To keep my brain sharp, I read a book by Thich Nhat Hanh called *No Mud, No Lotus*. In Buddhism, the lotus flower is a powerful symbol of growth and enlightenment, as its beautiful petals bloom forth from long stalks that grow up out of muddy waters. Even when things look dark, muddy, and hopeless, the lotus flower reminds us that it is still possible for beauty and happiness to emerge from a dark, muddy place.

Just as there can be no lotus without mud, I thought, without death there can be no life. You are dying from the moment you are

155

born. In *No Mud, No Lotus*, Hanh tells us, "It is actually very pleasant to die, which is also to live." Every second, cells within us die and new cells are born. Permanence is an illusion. The way to find happiness in this life, I have slowly learned, is not to free myself from suffering, but to embrace it and change my perspective in a way that lets suffering become the mud from which a lotus flower can bloom forth. When life piles on the mud, let's grow our own damn flowers from it.

After recovering at my parents' house for a week or so after surgery, I returned to my own apartment and began to experience the strange new reality of social distancing. I returned to work full time ten days after my second surgery, although, given my high-risk status, my work again consisted of virtual telemedicine appointments from home. As the pandemic continued in full force outside, I spent my recovery relatively isolated from the world.

Practicing telemedicine during the pandemic meant that I spent most of my days on the phone with patients reassuring them that they would recover from the virus. It was nice to be working again but also emotionally draining. During the day, I helped patients with their health concerns. In the evenings, I reflected on my own health concerns. There was no escape.

A week into my second surgical recovery, I felt tired, weak, and hopeless. After my first craniotomy, I had been constantly surrounded by family and friends. I'd had my night mistresses around me with food, gifts, and jokes. There had really been no time to feel lonely. This time, however, I spent most days alone in my apartment. My parents stopped by to deliver food, but I often refused others' help due to fears of spreading the virus.

Physically, recovery from my second craniotomy was easier than my first; emotionally, however, it was much worse. Craniotomies are intense surgeries and can cause emotional irritation, which I find fascinating. In a simple way, I think of it like this: If you have surgery on your knee, you have to teach your leg to stand again. If you have surgery on your brain, you have to teach your brain how to control your emotions again.

I was finally getting a handle on the waves of sadness and hopelessness that were my fun surgical side effects when I got an unexpected call from Dr. Lenn to "review my pathology results." I knew this was not a good sign.

To review, I had been diagnosed two months prior with a grade two or three glioma, otherwise known as an astrocytoma, an incurable but treatable brain cancer. Dr. Lenn spoke softly in a tone I knew meant nothing good. "Your surgical pathology shows your tumor was understaged on the biopsy. This time, it came back as fully grade three, an anaplastic astrocytoma."

"Grade three? Did it get worse in the past two months, or was it always a grade three?" I asked.

"We don't know," Dr. Lenn said. "Unfortunately, grade three gliomas are treated with chemotherapy and radiation. Surgery alone is not enough."

"So you're telling me I have malignant brain cancer and I need to start chemotherapy and radiation now, in the middle of a global pandemic?" I responded.

"Unfortunately, yes, I am," she said matter-of-factly.

"Well, no better time!" I joked. I don't think she understood my humor.

Two months prior, I had been a healthy young woman on a magical, independent adventure in Thailand. One month prior, I had been told I had a low-grade brain tumor with a life expectancy of perhaps twenty years after surgery, with no anticipated need for chemotherapy or radiation therapy. Now, two brain surgeries later, I had been told I had malignant, aggressive brain cancer.

"I know we can't know for sure, but statistically, what is my new estimated life expectancy?" I asked her.

"Five to ten years, statistically," she told me.

Delivering this news was like telling a knee-surgery patient she has to run a marathon before her knee is fully healed. My emotionally recovering brain had a hard time processing and accepting this news. *Five to ten years. OK, so it will essentially be a miracle if I make it to forty.*

I will likely never be able to have children. I will finally be settled into my career right around the time I have to enter a nursing home. "I guess I don't need to keep contributing to my 401K," I joked.

I thought about the Dalai Lama's words: "With our mind we create our own world." When I let my mind be consumed by sadness, socially isolating myself in a dark room crying about chemotherapy in the midst of a pandemic, the world I created was scary, lonely, horrifying, and unfair.

I decided to take a walk outside, letting my mind fill with thoughts of warmer days ahead, and my outlook changed. My world became lighter, brighter, and full of joy. I initially saw chemotherapy and radiation as a horrifying fire-breathing dragon looking at me, just a small paper doll about to be totally destroyed. Yet "with our mind we create our own world." So I changed my mind. I decided that I preferred to be the fire-breathing dragon. Cancer and the terrifying treatments that come with it could be the stupid little paper dolls, cowering for their lives. Time to burn, baby.

32

OK, enough surprises already

Suffering didn't make me more fearful; it made me more real.

—Ram Dass

Well, let me just say the news got worse from there. It doesn't even seem possible, but it's true. It was like I was bobbing in an ocean with an unrelenting storm around me, momentarily catching my breath only to be submerged yet again by an even bigger, scarier wave.

I accepted my fate of chemotherapy and radiation relatively quickly and, within a week, found myself back at the hospital for my radiation therapy simulation session, a pretreatment experience that I will describe as the worst spa day of my life.

To begin my spa treatment, I was ushered into a basement lobby where I sat next to three other radiation oncology patients. One woman, Milly, sat down a few seats over from me and eyed me sadly. "You just starting, honey? Don't worry, it's not so bad. I only have five treatments left to go. What are you in for?"

I felt as though we were inmates together, discussing our sentences even though we didn't really feel we were guilty. "Brain cancer. I'm here for my sim session today," I told her.

"Oh, sweetheart, you'll be fine," Milly cooed at me. She lifted up a bandana around her forehead, exposing sunburnt and blistering skin underneath. "This might happen to you; the radiation burns sometimes. Don't worry, though; it doesn't hurt, and a little coconut oil will calm your skin right down," she told me.

"Milly, we're ready for you!" a therapist called into the lobby.

"Bye, honey—good luck with everything," she told me, leaving me alone in the lobby, awaiting my sentencing.

As my appointment time arrived, I was brought to an examination room where a radiation oncologist reviewed my history and discussed the side effects of radiation treatment. "You will experience hair loss, scalp irritation, and fatigue. Many people experience memory loss, but we'll start you on a medication to try to prevent that." I nodded, at a loss for words.

"Many people develop eye cataracts, hearing loss, and secondary brain cancers ten or so years after their radiation treatment. It's not always the case, but we have to let you know in advance."

I sat there, alone in the clinic room (no visitors allowed during the pandemic), listening to my sentence. "*Guilty. Sentenced to ten years, but she likely won't live more than that anyways,*" I imagined the doctor thinking.

I thought about how I once would have been nervous at the prospect of cataracts, hearing loss, or another cancer; yet, with a life expectancy of "statistically five to ten years," what good was it to worry about a theoretical problem that wouldn't affect me until my body was long gone? "OK, let's do the damn thing." I told the doc. "Please preserve my memory; that's all I ask."

"I'll do my best," he told me.

With that, it was time for the spa treatment. I was brought across the hallway into a cold, quiet windowless room with a metal table in the middle of a large, donut-shaped MRI machine.

The radiation therapists in the room told me that we would now be making a mold of my head. "We'll have you lie on the table for about thirty minutes. During that time, you will keep your eyes closed and you will feel a very hot piece of plastic draped across your face. This plastic will slowly harden around your face, creating a mask that we can hook your head into during every radiation treatment," they told me.

As burning-hot plastic was draped across my face, I lay on the cold table with my eyes tightly shut, trying to imagine how good my pores would look after this very expensive, uncomfortable facial.

"That was one of the worst spa experiences of my life! But it was fascinating," I joked to the therapists before I left.

"Before you head out," they told me, "you will need one last MRI scan so we can line up the margins of the radiation treatment with the exact way your brain looks right now." Another MRI scan complete, I was finally free to head home.

Not minutes after I stepped inside my apartment, my phone rang. It was the radiation oncology office. *That's odd,* I thought.

It was my radiation oncologist, Dr. Anderson.* "Courtney, I have some bad news for you," he told me abruptly.

"OK, go ahead," I said, wondering what could possibly have happened in the last thirty minutes.

"The MRI scan you had at the end of the day today showed rapid tumor growth since your surgery. You have nearly seven centimeters of new tumor in your brain compared to two weeks ago. I called Dr. Clair and Dr. Lenn immediately after I saw the results, and we are all stumped."

"Excuse me? How could it possibly have grown that quickly?" I asked, heart racing, holding back tears.

"We don't know, to be very honest. Our worry is that your tumor has already progressed to a secondary glioblastoma," he said.

"Oh my god. So what now?"

"In a way, it's good we know this now. I will change my radiation plans to target a larger area of your brain, and we will do everything we can to get this tumor under control. I'm sorry to tell you this," Dr. Anderson said.

I thanked him and hung up, sitting down on the dog fur–coated carpet of my living room, sobbing uncontrollably. *Well, fuck,* was all I could think. There it was, the biggest wave yet, the wave that pulled me under the surface of the water and threatened to drown me once and for all. All I could think was, *What do I tell my family?*

I couldn't tell my family or friends in person due to the pandemic, so one by one, I called my loved ones and spoke the word "glioblastoma" into the phone. I listened to them all cry, every single one of them, as I cried into the phone with them.

As Steph picked up the phone and listened with the calm grace of a physician trained to hear bad news, I found myself sobbing into the phone. "Steph, I don't think I can be alone right now. We're supposed to social distance, but I need someone to come over."

Steph arrived at my apartment with a safe surgical mask on within twenty minutes, holding ice cream and wine, pulling me into a non–socially distanced hug and crying with me all evening.

At that point, I was not yet able to see the positives of my situation. I was not able to deal with the huge amount of suffering I suddenly felt. I was sad. I was terrified.

Between calls and sobs, I saw Thich Nhat Hanh's *No Mud, No Lotus* sitting on my coffee table. I thought of my perspective just a few days before. No mud, no lotus. No resilience, no recovery.

That day, I felt knee deep in mud. The mud was so high I must have stepped on the little lotus blossom without even seeing it. Sometimes, there is just too much damn mud.

I wondered, how can we clear the mud to see the happy little lotus blossoms emerging from below?

33

Run away

*I don't exercise to get fit or healthier, I do it to enjoy
being alive ... With each movement I do, I feel how
wonderful it is that I can still do it. Exercising ... I enjoy
having a body; I enjoy being alive. I accept life and
my body just as it is, and I feel so much gratitude.*

—Thich Nhat Hanh

The day after learning I might have a glioblastoma, I ran a 5K.
I know for many people that's basically nothing, but I am not a
runner. I have always despised running. I love fitness, but with
gyms closed during the pandemic, I had to resort to alternatives.
Following the Dalai Lama's advice, I decided to change my perspective by getting outside to see the huge, amazing world still turning
around me. Whenever a negative running thought would pop into
my head, essentially every other step, I would tell myself, "You are
nine days post–brain surgery and your legs work—use them!"

Every few seconds I would forget this motivational message and
again internally complain about running. But then I would think,
*You might be too tired to run for months once chemotherapy starts—do it
now!* and I would run faster. By the time I stopped, I had run 5K.
I had never run that far in my life, not before the cancer diagnosis
and definitely not after.

There had been many surprises in my life recently—divorce,
cancer, two brain surgeries, a pandemic. Yet the most surprising
event of all may have been the day that I became a runner. I could

not explain this illogical development. This may have been the first sign that I did indeed have brain cancer; I had lost my mind.

I've always been studious; I got many A grades, except in physical education. I failed PE in elementary school. I was always the sad last-place mile-run finisher. I switched to online PE in high school. It was as much of a joke as it sounds. I don't like to fail.

I tried to remember there are simple ways to be mindful in our day-to-day lives. Mindfulness does not require you to sit in silent meditation, or even to sit anywhere. Instead, it simply requires you to live in the moment and appreciate the moment for what it is. Brushing your teeth? Do that mindfully. Eating dinner? Do that mindfully too. Exercising? Yes, even that.

Life felt happier when I decided to accept life and my body just as they are.

If you can still breathe, enjoy the moment of breathing.

If you can still eat, enjoy every bite.

If you can still walk, enjoy each and every step.

If you can still smile, enjoy smiling. Fortunately, by the time I write these words, I'm up to 95 percent of a normal smile. I'm grateful for being able to smile a bit bigger as every day goes by.

Turns out, even if you flunked PE class, there is still hope for you. Accept your body for what it can do, and what it can't. Try to enjoy all the moments—the moments to sit, to think, to experience simply being alive. These magical moments are limited for all of us.

Remember that Thich Nhat Hanh tells us, "I accept life and my body just as it is, and I feel so much gratitude." This is not an easy thing to do, and I have to work on it every single day. But I truly believe that if you can have this compassion for yourself, it becomes much easier to have this compassion for others. That's all this life is really about.

Silly little glioblastoma can't stop me from running a 5K, damnit, I thought.

34

Difficult gifts

*Every day when you wake up you should try to
think, I am fortunate to be alive. I have a precious
human life. I am not going to waste it.*

—the Dalai Lama

In *The Book of Joy,* the Dalai Lama and Archbishop Desmond Tutu quote Brother David Steindl-Rast, a Catholic-Benedictine monk known for his work with Christian-Buddhist interfaith dialogue, about being grateful for all gifts we are given, whether or not they seem positive or negative at face value.

Brother David says, "It is not happiness that makes us grateful. It is gratefulness that makes us happy . . . Every moment is a gift . . . the gift within every gift is the opportunity it offers us. Most often it is the opportunity to enjoy it, but sometimes a *difficult* gift is given to us and that can be an opportunity to rise to the challenge."

I loved this strange juxtaposition as soon as I first read it. A difficult gift—how fascinating. This made me think, how often do we think of challenges or stressful situations as gifts? I definitely had not seen them this way before. Undergoing chemotherapy and radiation mid-pandemic, I thought, *Thank you, life, for this difficult gift. I can't promise I won't want the gift receipt, but I guess I'll try it out first before I complain too much. Maybe I'll end up actually liking something about it.*

In my mind, I compared this idea to the recent Christmas when I'd unwrapped a 5,000-piece puzzle. Even though all I'd wanted to do was complain about how I'd never have the time or interest to do something so awful, one day, a pandemic came along that trapped me inside my home and made me realize, *Thank goodness I got that awful puzzle last year. What a fantastic, difficult gift.*

I also thought this concept of difficult gifts could relate to the unexpected ending of a relationship: romantic, friendly, or on a grander scale involving the unexpected, untimely death of a loved one. When you lose a loved one in any of these scenarios, you might find yourself wondering, "Why, cruel world, did you introduce me to someone who brought happiness into my life if you knew you would later take that person away?" As a physician, I have felt this pain in a different sense when faced with the loss of a patient. Ironically, I now find myself having these thoughts about myself and how my own eventual death will impact others. I hope that someday, when I am gone, my illness and death can be seen as difficult gifts rather than burdens. I have always loved puzzles.

In searching for the gratitude while facing the difficult gift of malignant brain cancer, I came across a quote by another fabulous spiritual teacher, Pema Chödrön. Pema Chödrön is a Buddhist nun, teacher, and prolific writer. She has said, "When we think something is going to give us misery, we don't know. Letting there be room for not knowing is the most important thing of all."

Thank you, Pema. Thank you, Buddhism. Thank you, life, for these difficult gifts. Difficult gifts bring so many more opportunities for personal, emotional, and spiritual growth than any easy gift could. You never know when you might need a pandemic puzzle in the closet.

35

Make a list and throw it out

We often see the light everywhere but where we are, and chase after what we think we lack, only to find humbly it was with us all along.

—Mark Nepo

Around one week after my diagnosis of possible glioblastoma, I waited for my first chemotherapy and radiation session and wondered if I should start making a "bucket list." I sat down with a pen and paper. All I could think to put on it was travel: Bali, South America, Africa, Australia. Given the pandemic, unfortunately, I knew I had to be realistic about the fact that travel might not be the best thing to put on my bucket list. There was a chance my cancer would progress quite quickly. Although I hoped to have many more beautiful adventures in this lifetime, I couldn't be sure.

I reflected on Mark Nepo's words: we often find beauty everywhere but where we are until we realize this beauty was actually with us all along. In this reflection, I realized that my bucket list was all wrong. Sure, travel is wonderful. I hope I can see much more of the world. However, even if I don't get to check all those travel destinations off my list, that's OK too. I realized that day that my bucket list is already complete; in a sense, it has been complete all along.

The things on my list that are really important to me are the things I have been doing all my life—building strong relationships with friends and family, learning, teaching, loving. I became a doctor (likely in spite of a brain tumor, since I've probably had this thing for a while). I've traveled to beautiful places; I've eaten wonderful, indulgent food and drunk delicious wine. Although I don't have a human child, I have a fur child I love very much. I have made incredible relationships with people who mean the world to me; I have a loving and supportive family; I've learned that life is about living in the moment and being grateful for what we have right now. That day, I decided I would continue to do all these things that mean so much to me with whatever time I had left, especially strengthening my relationships with friends and family.

Strengthening my relationships with the people I love is by far the most important thing on my bucket list. When faced with your own mortality, nothing rings quite so true as realizing that we chase after what we think we lack, only to realize too late that we already had it. I realized that day: don't just plan your bucket list, live it, every single day.

36

Living vs. surviving

I am very happy every time I touch the beauty of life around me. Sometimes I feel deeply moved because there are so many beautiful things around me and also inside me. Sometimes the trees are so beautiful, the sky is so clear ... There are people capable of loving, forgiving, and taking care of other people ... I am inspired by the beauty around me and by the capacity for loving around me.

—Thich Nhat Hanh

The first day of chemotherapy and radiation finally arrived. My treatment plan consisted of an oral chemotherapy agent, a poisonous pill I would take every night on my own at home for six weeks. During these same six weeks, I would drive myself to radiation therapy every day from Monday to Friday for thirty total sessions of radiation.

That Sunday night, I sat alone in my apartment and called my night mistresses to check in. "Hey ladies, how are you? I'm about to take some really cool drugs," I joked with them, swallowing my antinausea pill an hour before my chemotherapy was due.

"Let us know how it goes," Marisa and Kari told me. "We love you; you're a badass," Steph answered. Mentally ready for battle, I thanked my ladies of the night and let the antinausea pill kick in.

An hour later, nervous as hell, I opened up the double-wrapped chemotherapy bag and swallowed a huge yellow pill. Ready to sprint to the bathroom, I was surprised to realize that I felt fine. I went to bed uneventfully and woke up the next morning with no discomfort.

Radiation was scheduled to start that Monday morning. I drove myself to the hospital and sat in the empty radiation oncology lobby, mentally preparing for another horrendous day at the spa.

Sometimes, life seems full of waiting. Waiting for an appointment, waiting for social distancing to end, waiting for a promotion, waiting for our next vacation, waiting to meet the right partner, waiting for happily ever after—just waiting.

During the COVID-19 pandemic, the whole world suddenly felt an even grander sense of waiting. Each day, people around the world would wake up and wonder, "When will this end? When will I be able to see my family, hug my grandchildren again? When will I be able to go out to eat? When will I be able to get my hair cut, my nails done? When will I know the answers, so I can plan my life again?"

Imagine if this waiting, this wondering, this waking up day after day without answers on a timeline was going to go on for the rest of your life. Welcome to having incurable cancer! Sounds like fun, huh? Obviously kidding, it's a nightmare.

The pandemic brought about a very unique phenomenon: the whole world collectively feeling the unknown that a cancer patient feels every day, all at the same time. It's almost spooky how much you can all relate to me having gone through this, together.

Imagine living your entire life with this same sense of the unknown, thinking *When will…?*

When will stores reopen? When will my cancer progress again? When will I know if my chemotherapy worked? When will my next brain scan be? When will my MRI show that my treatment is working, or that it is not working? When will I need another surgery? When will I lose my ability to remember, eat, speak, walk, think? I decided that "When will . . ." was the single worst phrase in existence. No one can answer it.

I feel that there is a large difference between living and simply surviving. If we want to live, we have to find a way to switch "When will . . . ?" to "Today, I will . . ."

If you think I'm trying to say, "Just be happy; it's easy," I'm not. It is not easy. No one is simply happy all the time without suffering. It is normal to suffer; this is part of being human. Do we have to suffer? If so, how can we suffer a little less? How can we counter the suffering enough to continue truly living, not just surviving?

In the many lifetimes I feel I have lived since my first seizure in Thailand, I've realized that when I wake up and think "When will . . . ?" I suffer. When I switch this phrase to "Today, I will . . . [go for a run, call my friends, see my family, walk my dog, help a patient, write a book, cook a delicious meal, sit in the sun]," I am able to remember the beauty of life around me, and "When will . . ." doesn't really matter so much after all. Sometimes, it's more important to just enjoy the day.

"Courtney, we're ready for you now," the radiation therapist called, waking me from my daydream. I followed him back to the radiation treatment room, which held two huge radiation machines. The best way I can describe these machines would be akin to how a futuristic MRI machine might appear on another planet. I was told to lie down on a hard metal table, and my head was locked into the plastic cage made specially for me. My head locked in its cold, plastic mask, truly Hannibal Lecter–like, my therapists told me they would step out of the room and I would hear the machine turn on momentarily.

The hum of the radiation machine turning on became a very familiar noise over the upcoming six weeks. The treatment itself lasted around five minutes from start to finish. Around ninety seconds in, without fail, I always smelled a strong chlorine scent.

After my first treatment, I asked my therapists why there was such a strong smell. One of them smiled and said, "Oh, some people say that. There isn't actually a smell, but sometimes people smell a chlorine or ozone-like smell if the radiation hits their brains in a certain place." Whoa, this was spooky as hell to me. My brain had apparently invented an imaginary smell as it was being zapped with energy. I left the first radiation treatment frightened, realizing I would not only be locked into a plastic cage on a hard metal table alone every day, but would also feel like I was drowning in a highly chlorinated pool the entire time as well.

I was grateful for my recent, more relaxing spa experience in Thailand as I walked out of radiation, dreading the next twenty-nine sessions to come.

37

Unquenchable thirst

The difference between misery and happiness depends
on what we do with our attention. Do we, in the midst
of water, look for something elsewhere to drink?

—Sharon Salzberg

I woke up the next morning dreading the day ahead and realized I needed to change my perspective before driving myself back to session two of radiation therapy. Flipping through a book by Sharon Salzberg, I read the quote above, and it resonated with me.

For much of my life before cancer, I failed to see beauty and happiness around me while I searched for something better. When I read Salzberg's words, I pictured myself swimming in a beautiful, crystal-clear pool of fresh water—yet all I could think about was how thirsty I was, how much happier I would be if only I had a fancy bottle of water to drink.

As I reflected on this, I realized that many of us can likely relate to this feeling of wanting, looking for, hoping for something to drink even in the midst of water.

Salzberg goes on to say that "when we experience mental or physical pain, we often feel a sense of isolation, a disconnection from humanity and life. Our shame sets us apart in our suffering at the very times when we need most to connect."

Early on in this story, I told you that I went through a period of clinical depression in my second year of residency. When I wrote that in my very public blog, many of my friends reached out and told me how sorry they were for not noticing that I was going through this at the time. I hadn't even consciously registered that I did not tell my friends about this at the time. Thinking back, I believe I was embarrassed by my depression. I was too ashamed to tell anyone. Shame set me apart in my suffering. I realized then that I have no time for shame anymore. Life is short; stigma is stupid.

Working with patients during the recent pandemic, I noticed many of them developed significant depression and anxiety in the setting of social distancing, isolation, and a fear of the unknown. To help, the hospital system I worked for at the time created a virtual instant messaging system for patients to send quick questions to their physician. Most of the answers we provided were not medically challenging. I can't count the number of times I responded to a patient with, "Many of our patients have the same symptoms. I want to reassure you that . . ." I found that simple reassurance, sharing the knowledge that none of us are suffering in this life alone, is sometimes the best medicine we can give.

When you are suffering, I hope you will remember that you too are surrounded by water, by happiness, by love. Since my experience with depression, I have worked on finding mindfulness, finding happiness, with today, with now, with the water I'm already in the midst of.

The roller-coaster ride of my cancer diagnosis, first low grade, then malignant and aggressive, used to make me feel mental pain. Not depression, but sadness. When I felt sad, I found myself sinking into an "Oh, poor me, I'm so isolated, so disconnected" type of mindset.

When I realized one day that I had no time for shame, that I was not the only one in this world who suffered, I felt profound peace. I decided to refuse to feel shame about having real emotions. I refused to hide my suffering with cancer as I did with my depression. I wrote about it publicly, for all to read, because suffering is not a unique experience. Do not feel shame in this. We are not alone in our suffering.

One of my favorite mantras comes from Thich Nhat Hanh: "Darling, I am suffering. Please help." These six words can be very difficult to say, but sometimes they are the most important six words we can say. There is no shame in suffering.

I drove to radiation that day, reciting that mantra over and over again in my head. As I lay down on the table, mentally prepared to feel myself claustrophobically drowning in fictitious chlorine, I thought, *Darling, I am suffering. Please help.*

Even though no one responded out loud, I made it through that radiation session and another twenty-eight more. Instead of picturing myself drowning in a chlorinated pool, I began to meditate in the radiation cage. I imagined I was lying in a perfectly clean, recently sterilized meditation corner of a spa, waiting for a glorious facial treatment to begin.

38

Why worry?

*If a problem is fixable, if a situation is such that you can
do something about it, then there is no need to worry.
If it is not fixable, then there is no help in worrying.
There is no benefit in worrying whatsoever.*

—the Dalai Lama

Routine in place, I spent the next six weeks going back and forth from radiation treatments and slowly poisoning myself with nightly chemotherapy in hopes of a successful treatment response.

Every time I found my mind wandering into the past or into the future, I would reflect on one of my favorite Dalai Lama quotes, the one about worrying, or rather, not worrying, written above. For me, living my life without worry has become the most refreshing thing I have ever experienced.

I have cancer, that's true. Instead of worrying about it, I take a two-step approach based on the Dalai Lama's wise words above. First, I ask myself, "Is this problem fixable? Is there something I can do about it?" Yes; I can take chemotherapy and go to radiation. Unfortunately, because I am human, I naturally jump to another scary question: "What if these treatments don't work?" After a momentary panic, I move on to the second step.

Next, I remind myself that there is no benefit in worrying and ask myself the first question again. Thankfully, I've already answered that question. I am doing something to remedy the situation: chemotherapy and radiation. Good for me! So, you see, worrying has no place here.

The Dalai Lama said the words. I used his wisdom and applied it to my own life in the two-step approach outlined above. For me, it works wonders.

Because my brain tumor is on the right side of my brain, when it grows, it will affect the left side of my body. When this tumor grows, it will likely cause numbness and other sensory changes first, followed by muscle issues including possible left-sided paralysis. Even though emotionally this is hard to think about, I know from a medical standpoint these symptoms are likely to occur someday. Fortunately, my tumor is located far away from my speech and language-processing centers. I am hopeful my ability to speak and process language will be spared, but no one knows for sure.

I do not spend time worrying about these medical uncertainties. Instead, every single morning that I wake up with full function of my left arm and leg, I start my day smiling. When I wake up and realize I have no numbness or tingling on my left side, when I remember I still have the ability to pick up my coffee mug with my left hand and take a step forward with my left foot, I drink my delicious coffee and go for a walk outside with complete, pure joy. I can no longer take the physical abilities of my body for granted. A functioning body is something we should cherish and enjoy. We aren't promised unlimited time to appreciate the miraculous abilities our human body gives us.

Sometimes, I find my mind starts to wander into the future, the "When will . . ." questions flooding back in. When will I start to have numbness in my left leg? When will I no longer be able to walk? When will my treatment stop working? When will I leave this life? I can't answer these questions. Doctors can't answer these questions.

I think there is a reason no one can answer these questions.

Even if you can't directly relate to my personal issues, you might find yourself asking the universe similar questions.

"How long will I be healthy? How long will I be alive? Will I be in a bad accident and become paralyzed? When will this happen? Will I ever lose the ability to swallow, to eat? Will I lose my vision, my hearing, my speech? Will I lose my memory? When will I die?"

For me, it's even worse to think about these hypothetical scenarios affecting a family member or friend. "When will my loved one become sick? When will my loved one die? Will my loved one experience a horrific trauma, become paralyzed? Will he lose the ability to speak? Will she lose the ability to see? To hear? How long do I have on earth with her? What if this is less time than I think? Will I have to live without him? Will she have to live without me? Will we be sad when this happens? How will we survive without them?"

Do you find yourself feeling anxious even considering these questions? Do you find your heart starts racing or your palms start sweating? Do you feel your mind races ten steps ahead and imagines the worst possible outcomes to all these hypothetical scenarios? I think this is a natural way to feel.

When this happens to me, I return to my two-step approach to worrying. First, I ask, "Are any of these questions answerable? Are any of these problems fixable?" In many situations, the answer is no. Unfortunately, it's hard not to fall into the deep well of questions listed above, all of them without answers. When this happens, I perform the second step. I remind myself again and again that there is no benefit in worrying, and I ask myself the first question again. "Are any of these questions answerable? Are any of these problems fixable?" Nope. Well, shit. Now what?

Now, I reflect on what the Dalai Lama says about this situation: "If it is not fixable, then there is no help in worrying. There is no benefit in worrying whatsoever."

And with that, I stop worrying. I change "When will . . ." to

"Today, I will . . ." I use my left hand to drink my delicious, perfect sip of black dark-roast coffee, and I use my left leg to take another scary, exciting step forward into the mystery of this life. That's really all any of us can do, isn't it?

39

Lovingkindness

Through lovingkindness, everyone and
everything can flower again from within.

—Sharon Salzberg

When I started to lose my hair around two weeks into radiation, I felt strangely free, as if I were shedding my past, creating a new, more satisfying me. After I stood in the shower watching large clumps of brown hair fall out around me, I called Marisa and told her, "It's time. The hair must go."

As I drove to meet Marisa in a safe outdoor area with pandemic-appropriate masks on our faces, I realized that I could spend today feeling fear or acceptance. I chose to practice lovingkindness toward myself. I chose to thank my body and my mind for the great places they have taken me so far, despite the unexpected obstacles I had faced and still had yet to face. I chose to love myself despite my fear, or maybe in spite of my fear, because loving ourselves seems to be the best foundation we have for loving others. Loving others and having compassion (literally "to suffer with") for others is, I believe, the real purpose of this chaos we call life.

Marisa shaved my hair off that evening. Strand by strand, I felt myself shedding the layers of my previous life and embracing my new, kinder, more compassionate self with an open heart. Over the next six weeks, I completed thirty sessions of radiation and forty-two days of chemotherapy. I took an oral chemotherapy pill every night for a gentle pre-bedtime poisoning and drove myself to and from radiation every Monday through Friday for six full weeks. My family and friends were 100 percent supportive throughout this journey, yet the pandemic continued, and with it hospital visitor restrictions. I went through the entire ordeal physically alone.

Writing was therapeutic for me during this time. In fact, I wrote this book during those six weeks of treatment. As I write this sentence, I am entering my last week of treatment. I do not yet know if the treatment worked or not. Fortunately, I'm having a damn good time living my life regardless.

One of the four Buddhist brahma-viharas, or virtues, is called *mudita*, or sympathetic joy. Mudita is, in essence, the exact opposite of schadenfreude, pleasure derived from someone else's misfortune. Schadenfreude is the happiness we may secretly or not-so-secretly feel when we see others suffer. It sounds horrible, but we all do it.

Mudita, on the other hand, is pleasure derived from someone else's well-being, much more beautiful than schadenfreude. Probably the easiest way to describe mudita is to think of a parent's happiness when they see their child succeed. No jealously, just pure and simple joy.

After my cancer diagnosis, I found myself looking around at other people my age who were healthy, spending their afternoons at happy hour instead of radiation, getting married, having babies. I felt sorry for myself and irrationally irritated at the good fortune everyone else seemed to be having.

Sharon Salzberg describes this feeling more eloquently in her book *Lovingkindness*. She states, "We may look at someone else's achievements or someone else's happiness and find ourselves wishing that their status or condition might be diminished—as if thereby our own would be increased. This attitude of diminishing the happiness of others is based on considering happiness as a limited resource or commodity—the more someone else has, the less there is for me."

The inner scientific nerd in me wanted to research this idea. I came across an interesting research study from the *British Medical Journal* that actually found the opposite is true. A study called the *Dynamic spread of happiness in a large social network* (Fowler *et al.*, 2008) looked at precisely this question. The objective of this study was to observe if happiness can spread from person to person, and whether happiness can spread through social networks or not.

The results of this study found that happiness spreads like a virus. To quote the article, results showed that "the relationship between people's happiness extends up to three degrees of separation (for example, to the friend of one's friends' friends). People who are surrounded by many happy people and those who are central in the network are more likely to become happy in the future."

Scientifically, happiness is not a limited resource in any way; in fact, happiness may be contagious. Through mudita, sympathetic joy, I found that by finding pleasure in the happiness of others, I could in turn create happiness for myself. I call this being selfishly selfless.

Like a virus, once we start spreading happiness, it will quickly spread far and wide. Buddhists say this. Scientists say this. I say this too.

40

Impermanence can be beautiful

*Some people, sweet and attractive, and strong and
healthy, happen to die young. They are masters in
disguise teaching us about impermanence.*

—the Dalai Lama

In Buddhism, impermanence is a fundamental teaching. I often
meditate and reflect on the idea of impermanence, the constant
unalterable change of everything in our lives. As a scientist, I
equate this idea to that of entropy. The laws of thermodynamics
are, strangely, quite similar to the ideas taught in Buddhist philosophy. I guess it doesn't really matter who the teachers are; what
matters is that we are open to learn.

I promise that this chapter will not have a chemistry or physics
test at the end, but I do think these are interesting concepts to
think about. As a reminder, the first law of thermodynamics tells
us that energy cannot be created or destroyed. The second law
of thermodynamics speaks to what happens to energy when it is
transformed, since it cannot be created or destroyed. As energy is
transformed in an isolated system (essentially, our universe), some
of it is wasted. Entropy is essentially a measure of this wasted energy, or energy that is not available to do useful work. This wasted
energy leads to increased randomness, or disorder, of a system.

The second law of thermodynamics tells us that the total entropy, or disorder, of the universe is always increasing.

A simple way to think about the concept of entropy is to think about dumping one of your pandemic puzzle boxes out on a table. Will the pieces fall together in a nice, neat, complete puzzle? That would be incredible, but likely will not happen. It is easier for the universe to trend toward disorder than order, with puzzles and with our lives.

In other words, unpredictable change is always coming. From the smallest particles to our entire universe, everything moves toward messy, unexpected, disorderly change.

The Buddha reportedly said, "Nothing is permanent. Everything is subject to change. Being is always becoming."

Thich Nhat Hanh takes the concept of impermanence and tells us simply, "It is not impermanence that makes us suffer. What makes us suffer is wanting things to be permanent when they are not."

Emotions, physical health, age, relationships, praise, criticism, exciting news, difficult news; all these concepts are impermanent. Slow drivers in front of you, traffic jams, social distancing, sickness; all these things are impermanent too.

Many of us like to live in a bubble of stability, imagining that everything will stay exactly the same. I used to live in this bubble. It was safe and cozy inside. Then, the bubble burst. Entropy, impermanence, life came at me and taught me a crash course in reality that I wasn't necessarily prepared for.

The unfortunate thing is that permanence is fiction. Whether we read Buddhist teachings from 2,500 years ago or slightly more modern, scientifically validated laws of thermodynamics, we can see that really only one thing can live in our bubble of stability, and that thing is change. Fortunately, change can be beautiful too.

41

What are you waiting for in order to be happy?

"Qu'est-ce qu'on attend pour être heureux?"
(What are you waiting for in order to be happy?)
You can be happy right here and right now.

—Thich Nhat Hanh, reciting a French song

I finished six weeks of chemotherapy and radiation while a pandemic raged on around me. I finished radiation, serendipitously, the same day I finished my internal medicine residency. I took this as a good sign. My radiation therapists handed me my plastic head cage on the last day of treatment and joked that I could take it home as my "graduation cap." I laughed and hugged them goodbye.

That afternoon, I reflected on all that had happened over the past six months as I sat in my living room with my dog at my feet, drinking a mug of coffee, listening to raindrops flood the world outside. Looking out the window, I saw green leaves had appeared on trees overnight, blowing in the stormy wind, filled with new life. Spring was here.

My dog, Ridley, sat at my feet, terrified of the rain, eyes closed. Over the past few months, I've often wondered if she can sense that I am sick. I've heard that dogs can do this, and a quick medical literature search shows many scientific studies have demonstrated that some dogs can detect cancer with smell alone.

I don't know that I can give Ridley that much credit, but I can tell you that she acted as my guard dog those six months, never leaving my side. She sat at my feet while I was working, lay by my side while I was sleeping, and snuggled up close to me while I was writing. As the rain beat down around me, Ridley was in her usual position, lying dutifully at my feet, ready to protect me; yet as I looked at her face and watched her paws shake, I could tell she was also silently terrified of the storm around her.

As I watched her, I reflected on the uncanny similarities between all humans, and even animals. Day after day, we wake up and take our positions. We put on our best faces and ready ourselves physically and mentally to take on another day of our routines. We tell ourselves we can do this—this job, this challenge, this life—as long as we need to, yet we are also silently terrified as the unrelenting storm continues around us.

As I thought about this, I realized that even when the rain starts, it also stops eventually. Rain, like everything else in this beautiful and unexpected life, is impermanent. The clear sky is always waiting for us underneath.

42

Finding joy

Smile. Do not cry. This happened for a reason.

—Buddhist Monk, name unknown,
Thailand, January 2020

As long as I have left on this earth, I'll continue to look for joy, for happiness, for compassion. I am one small human being in a world of over seven billion human beings. All of us have a few things in common. We are born, we face challenges, we learn something, and we die. I think we can all find a little joy simply by accepting that we are all doing this dance together.

After finishing my first cycle of treatment, I had one glorious treatment-free month before my next MRI scan, which would show if the treatment had worked to stabilize the cancer or not. In the meantime, I figured I would go on a spontaneous adventure. As the pandemic continued, travel options were limited. However, roads were open and the sun was shining, so I packed up my bags and decided to visit my brother, Matt, and his fiancée at their home in Kansas.

I called my brother. "Matt, are you guys around this weekend? Crazy bald sister wants to come and visit you!"

"We're here. Come visit, that would be fantastic!" Matt told me. I quickly packed my bag, dropped Ridley off with her dog dad, James, and threw my suitcase into the trunk of my small car. As I leaned over the open trunk to position the suitcase, I noticed a book sticking out of the corner of my bag. *The Universe in a Single*

Atom stuck its curious head out of my suitcase, reminding me in no subtle terms of the lessons it had taught me over the past six months.

There I stood, preparing to leave for another journey, with less hair on my head, less worry in my mind, and more love in my heart than the journey I'd taken six short months before.

Smile. Do not cry. This happened for a reason. Thank you, wise monk, for teaching me the simplest, most beautiful lesson I've ever heard. It took me twenty-nine years to learn it, and I have to teach it to myself again every single day, but I have yet to find a lesson more worthwhile to learn.

I may be dying, but I'm also truly living—fully, beautifully, and gratefully—all the way to the end.

Resources

- National Suicide Prevention Lifeline: 1-800-273-8255

- Advance Care Planning and Healthcare Directives:

  ° I would be remiss if I did not encourage you to fill out your own advance care plan or health-care directive. The forms are free to fill out and available online. They are slightly different in every state, so please discuss them with your primary care provider. Download, print, and fill out these forms today. Do not wait until you are too sick to do this.

- Documentary: *Love and Bananas* by Ashley Bell is a fascinating documentary about the oftentimes horrific plight of Asian elephants and offers a chance to see the remarkable new life an ethical elephant sanctuary offers these magnificent creatures.

- Books: Many wonderful books taught and inspired me throughout the creation of this memoir. Some of my favorites include the following:

  ° *The Universe in a Single Atom: The Convergence of Science and Spirituality* by His Holiness the Dalai Lama and Archbishop Desmond Tutu

  ° *The Book of Joy* by His Holiness the Dalai Lama

  ° *An Open Heart: Practicing Compassion in Everyday Life* by His Holiness the Dalai Lama

  ° *The Art of Happiness* by His Holiness the Dalai Lama

  ° *The Path to Tranquility* by His Holiness the Dalai Lama

- ° *Advice on Dying and Living a Better Life* by His Holiness the Dalai Lama

- ° *How to Expand Love: Widening the Circle of Loving Relationships* by His Holiness the Dalai Lama

- ° *No Mud, No Lotus* by Thich Nhat Hanh

- ° *The Art of Living* by Thich Nhat Hanh

- ° *How to Love* by Thich Nhat Hanh

- ° *Peace Is Every Step* by Thich Nhat Hanh

- ° *Going Home: Jesus and Buddha as Brothers* by Thich Nhat Hanh

- ° *Lovingkindness: The Revolutionary Art of Happiness* by Sharon Salzberg

- ° *Faith: Trusting Your Own Deepest Experience* by Sharon Salzberg

- ° *Radical Acceptance: Embracing Your Life with the Heart of a Buddha* by Tara Brach, PhD

- ° *Living Beautifully with Uncertainty and Change* by Pema Chödrön

- ° *When Things Fall Apart* by Pema Chödrön

- ° *The Book of Awakening* by Mark Nepo

Shari Fleming Photography

Courtney Burnett is an internal medicine physician living and working in Saint Paul, Minnesota. She is actively involved in brain cancer advocacy and outreach. This is her first book. Read her continuously updated blog at www.elephantlotusbraintumor.com. Contact Courtney at courtney.burnett264@gmail.com or follow her on Instagram (courtneyjburnett) or Twitter (@CourtneyB_MD).

Speaking engagements

Courtney is available for speaking engagements, workshops, and fundraising events. She can speak about her experience living as both patient and physician, finding joy despite unexpected challenges, practicing mindfulness, and making the most of every moment even when faced with a terminal illness before the age of thirty.

Courtney has spoken about her experiences in the medical community and with various brain cancer advocacy and awareness groups. Her style is open, honest, funny, conversational, and inclusive.

If you're interested in booking Courtney for a speaking event, please email courtney.burnett264@gmail.com or reach her on her blog at www.elephantlotusbraintumor.com/speaking.